RAND Center for Catastrophic Risk
Management and Compensation

Flood Insurance in New York City Following Hurricane Sandy

Lloyd Dixon, Noreen Clancy, Bruce Bender, Aaron Kofner,
David Manheim, Laura Zakaras

T0308381

Prepared for the New York City Mayor's Office of
Long-Term Planning and Sustainability

The research described in this report was sponsored by the New York City Mayor's Office of Long-Term Planning and Sustainability and conducted in the Center for Catastrophic Risk Management and Compensation within RAND Justice, Infrastructure, and Environment.

Library of Congress Cataloging-in-Publication Data is available for this publication.
ISBN: 978-0-8330-8263-3

The RAND Corporation is a nonprofit institution that helps improve policy and decisionmaking through research and analysis. RAND's publications do not necessarily reflect the opinions of its research clients and sponsors.

Support RAND—make a tax-deductible charitable contribution at www.rand.org/giving/contribute.html

RAND® is a registered trademark.

Cover image: A man walks through flood waters to survey damage from Hurricane Sandy in the New Dorp Beach neighborhood of the Staten Island borough of New York, November 1, 2012 (Reuters/Lucas Jackson).

© Copyright 2013 RAND Corporation

This document and trademark(s) contained herein are protected by law. This representation of RAND intellectual property is provided for noncommercial use only. Unauthorized posting of RAND documents to a non-RAND website is prohibited. RAND documents are protected under copyright law. Permission is given to duplicate this document for personal use only, as long as it is unaltered and complete. Permission is required from RAND to reproduce, or reuse in another form, any of our research documents for commerical use. For information on reprint and linking permissions, please see the RAND permissions page (www.rand.org/pubs/permissions.html).

RAND OFFICES
SANTA MONICA, CA • WASHINGTON, DC
PITTSBURGH, PA • NEW ORLEANS, LA • JACKSON, MS • BOSTON, MA
DOHA, QA • CAMBRIDGE, UK • BRUSSELS, BE
www.rand.org

Preface

This report provides the most-comprehensive data to date on flood insurance coverage in New York City both before and after Hurricane Sandy made landfall on October 29, 2012. It also examines the consequences of changes to the National Flood Insurance Program and the update of the Federal Emergency Management Agency's flood insurance rate map for the city's residents in the wake of Hurricane Sandy. It is hoped that this work will provide information needed for discussions of proposed policy options for mitigating risk and making insurance premiums more affordable in the future. The research was supported by the New York City Mayor's Office of Long-Term Planning and Sustainability, and initial results provided background data on flood insurance for the City's recent report, *A Stronger, More Resilient New York*, released June 2013.[1]

RAND Center for Catastrophic Risk Management and Compensation

The RAND Center for Catastrophic Risk Management and Compensation conducts research and seeks to identify policies, strategies, and other measures that have the potential to reduce the adverse social and economic effects of natural and manmade catastrophes by

- improving incentives to reduce future losses
- providing just compensation to those suffering losses while appropriately allocating liability to responsible parties
- helping affected individuals, businesses, and communities to recover quickly
- avoiding unnecessary legal, administrative, and other transaction costs.

The center is part of RAND Justice, Infrastructure, and Environment, a division of the RAND Corporation dedicated to improving policy and decisionmaking in a wide range of policy domains, including civil and criminal justice, infrastructure protec-

---

[1] City of New York, "A Stronger, More Resilient New York," June 2013.

tion and homeland security, transportation and energy policy, and environmental and natural resources policy.

Questions or comments about this report and requests from more information about the Center for Catastrophic Risk Management and Compensation should be sent to Lloyd Dixon (Lloyd_Dixon@rand.org). For more information on RAND Justice, Infrastructure, and Environment, see http://www.rand.org/jie or contact the director, Debra Knopman (Debra_Knopman@rand.org).

Contents

Figures

Tables

Summary

On the anniversary of Hurricane Sandy, many residents of New York City are still struggling to rebuild their homes, businesses, and lives. A year after the storm, they have learned that their recovery faces a new hurdle: changes in the flood insurance market that are likely to bring about much higher premiums for many residents living near the coast. How bad is the news? What can be done in response?

To understand the dimensions of this problem, the New York City Mayor's Office of Long-Term Planning and Sustainability asked the RAND Corporation to analyze the changes in the flood insurance landscape in New York City following Hurricane Sandy and what these changes will mean to the city's residents and businesses. This report provides the most-comprehensive answers to date to several important questions:

- What did flood insurance coverage in New York City look like before Hurricane Sandy, and what effect has Hurricane Sandy had on flood insurance markets?
- What are the consequences for New York City of changes in the National Flood Insurance Program (NFIP) and updates in the flood-risk maps for the city?
- How can policymakers help people in high-risk areas of New York City deal with major increases in insurance premiums?
- What key data should be collected, and what analyses should be done to evaluate potential responses?

New York City residents and businesses can buy flood insurance from the federal government through the NFIP or in the private market. The NFIP is the dominant source of flood insurance for homeowners and smaller residential properties and businesses. The NFIP was established in 1968 and is currently administered by the Federal Emergency Management Agency (FEMA). For decades, flood insurance has been mandated for any structure located in a high-risk area in the United States that has a mortgage from a federally regulated lender (i.e., the mandatory purchase requirement). High-risk areas are defined as areas in the 100-year floodplain—that is, those areas that have a 1-percent annual chance of flooding. Two recent changes, however, both planned long before Hurricane Sandy struck, are being implemented at the same time as storm victims in New York City are struggling to rebuild. They are both intended

xii   Flood Insurance in New York City Following Hurricane Sandy

to put the federal program, which has accumulated billions of dollars of cost overruns since Hurricane Katrina in 2005, on a stronger financial footing by moving toward more risk-based premiums.

The first of these changes, the Biggert-Waters Flood Insurance Reform Act of 2012 (BW-12) (Pub. L. 112-141), eliminates the subsidies that existed for some classes of structures. It also phases out the grandfathering of certain structures when flood maps are updated: In the past, if a new map located these structures in a higher-risk flood zone, owners would still be able to pay premiums that are based on the prior map.

The second change is the update of the FEMA map that defines the flood-risk areas in New York. Flood insurance rate maps (FIRMs) identify areas at risk of flooding, including high-risk areas. The underlying analysis and mapping of flood risk for New York City had not been updated since FEMA released its first map for the city in 1983. Preliminary versions of the new map, released in June 2013 and expected to be finalized in 2015, reveal an expanded floodplain that includes approximately twice as many structures in the high-risk zones and greater flood depths for those structures already in the high-risk zones.

Although we provide estimates of the premium increases that will result from these changes, exactly what those changes will be and when they might begin will depend on how FEMA implements certain provisions of BW-12 and whether proposals to delay or reduce some of the premium increases in the act move forward in Congress.

How Well Insured Were Those in New York City for Flood Damage When Hurricane Sandy Hit?

Figure S.1 compares the flood map that was in effect when the storm hit (dated from 2007 but only minimally updated since it was first released in 1983) and the flood map released in June 2013, called the Preliminary Work Map. We describe here the flood insurance coverage at the time of the storm for structures in New York City, when the 2007 map defined the high-risk zones.

Number of Residents and Businesses in High-Risk Flood Zones

At the time Hurricane Sandy hit the coast, there were 35,700 structures in these high-risk areas, which accounted for 162,700 residential units. Perhaps surprising for a dense, urban area like New York City is that most of these structures (72 percent) were homes for one to four families. Eighty percent of structures in the high-risk areas were built before 1983, when the first flood map was issued for the city. In other words, these structures were built without the benefit of today's building standards and understanding of flood risk.

Figure S.1
Areas at High Risk for Coastal Flooding

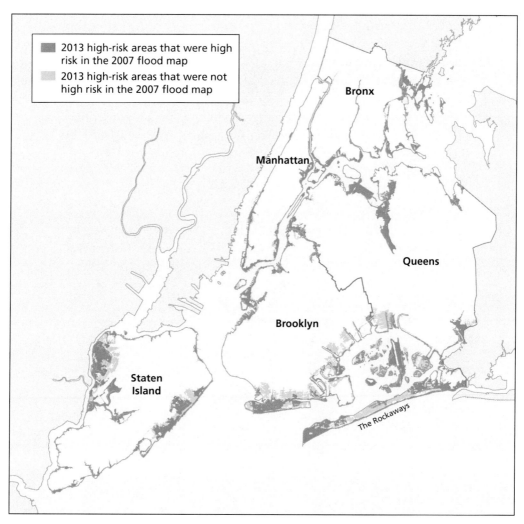

SOURCES: FEMA Map Service Center data for 2007; Risk Assessment, Mapping, and Planning Partners (RAMPP), "Preliminary Work Map Data," June 18, 2013.
NOTE: Areas subject to riverine flooding are not included.
RAND RR328-S.1

Proportion of Residences and Businesses with Flood Insurance

We estimate that 55 percent of the one- to four-family homes in the high-risk areas on the 2007 map had federal flood insurance on the eve of Hurricane Sandy. Approximately three-quarters of these homes are subject to the mandatory purchase requirement; of these, about two-thirds have flood coverage. Among homeowners not required to buy coverage, the take-up rate is only about 20 percent. Because important data are missing, future analysis is needed to characterize the take-up rates for multifamily residential buildings (which would include large apartment buildings and condominiums) and mixed-use buildings (those with both commercial and residential zoning). Most residential *units* in the high-risk areas (78 percent), on the other hand, are found in multifamily or mixed-use dwellings.

Nearly all very large commercial firms carry flood insurance purchased from private insurers. Interviews with industry experts estimated the share to be 80 to 90 percent (not just in high-risk areas but overall) because large firms tend to purchase inclusive manuscript policies. Large insured firms typically do not buy federal flood insurance except occasionally to reduce a high deductible on a manuscript policy.

By contrast, very few small firms have private flood insurance coverage: Experts estimated the share to be as low as 5 to 10 percent. If small firms buy coverage at all, they tend to rely on the NFIP.

Gaps in Coverage

Hurricane Sandy revealed gaps in the flood insurance system that should be given priority attention in efforts to improve New York City's resiliency in the next event. For residential structures with NFIP coverage, the most-important gaps are

- limited basement coverage
- lack of coverage for additional living expenses
- lack of coverage for damage due to earth movement resulting from flooding.

For commercial structures with NFIP coverage, the most-important gaps are

- limited basement coverage
- lack of business-interruption or business-expense coverage
- inadequate coverage for mixed-use buildings.

For commercial structures with private flood insurance coverage, the most-important gaps are

- lack of coverage for business interruption or extra expenses in cases in which there was no physical flood damage on the premises
- varying coverage for street and area closures imposed by civil authorities.

Hurricane Sandy's Impact on Private Insurance Markets

Hurricane Sandy resulted in substantial claim payments by private insurers for wind as well as flood damage. At an estimated $18.8 billion (including losses outside New York City), insured losses due to Hurricane Sandy were roughly half those for Hurricane Katrina. This figure does not include NFIP claim payments and is likely dominated by wind-related losses. Even though claim payments were substantial, Hurricane Sandy's impact on the overall U.S. insurance market appears to be modest. Prices for commercial property coverage (excluding flood), business-interruption, and general liability insurance appear to have been little affected by Hurricane Sandy both nationwide and in the Northeast. However, our investigation did indicate that premiums for flood insurance purchased from private insurers for many commercial properties in New York City's high-risk zones have increased substantially since Hurricane Sandy. For buildings that experienced a loss, increases of 35 to 40 percent are not uncommon. Private insurers also appear to be reducing their exposure in high-risk areas by reducing policy limits or dropping flood coverage altogether. Flood coverage is still available, but a commercial property owner will likely need to piece together coverage from a larger number of insurers than before Hurricane Sandy.

Consequences of Changes in the National Flood Insurance Program

The map that FEMA released in June 2013 (see Figure S.1) greatly expands the city's high-risk areas and nearly doubles the number of structures and residents in those areas, as shown in Figure S.2. Added to the high-risk areas are structures that were not built to floodplain standards because the floodplain building standards do not apply to areas outside the current high-risk areas. As a result, 90 percent of the 67,400 structures in the expanded high-risk areas have not been built to floodplain standards. In the event of another major storm, according to the new map, the flood depth in the existing high-risk areas is also estimated to be greater. The changes vary across different parts of the city, but increases of 2 to 4 feet are common. These changes reflect a realization that flood risk in the city is higher than previously thought. And the risk will likely increase over time, putting more structures at risk because the updated map does not capture the consequences of future sea-level rise or the greater frequency of severe storms that might result from climate change.

Many more homeowners will also be *required* to purchase insurance. We estimate that the number of one- to four-family structures subject to the mandate will roughly double to 34,500. Only about 35 percent of these homes had flood insurance as of October 2012.

Effects on Insurance Premiums

As a consequence of the expanded flood map and the phase-out of premium subsidies and rate grandfathering enacted in 2012, local residents will face escalating costs for flood insurance. To estimate the dimension of these increases, we developed plausible scenarios for how the premiums might change with the adoption of the new flood map, assuming that it is similar to the preliminary map that has not yet been formally adopted. In some cases, premiums increased by $1,000 to $2,000 per year. As stipu-

Figure S.2
Number of Structures in High-Risk Areas of the Preliminary Work Map Compared with Those on the 2007 Flood Map

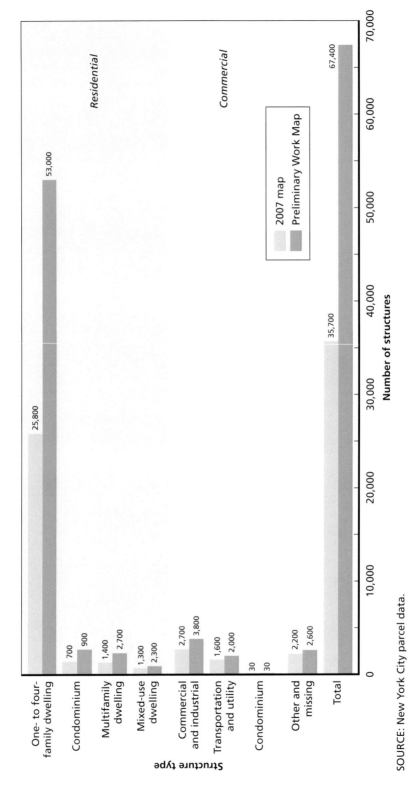

SOURCE: New York City parcel data.
NOTE: Numbers have been rounded to the nearest hundred. Because of rounding, bars might not sum precisely. The Preliminary Work Map does not identify regions subject to riverine, as opposed to coastal, flooding. However, the missing areas are likely to be relatively moderate in size. In the 2007 flood map, only 2.7 square miles of the 33 square miles in the high-risk flood areas (8 percent) were subject to riverine flooding. The data for the preliminary map did not include areas subject to riverine flooding, but such an exclusion should not have much effect on the findings.
RAND RR328-S.2

lated in BW-12, such increases will be phased in over five years in many cases. In other cases, however, premiums would not change: The act allows primary residences that were built before the first flood map was issued in an area (which, for New York City, was November 1983) to retain their subsidized rates. To qualify, these homes must not have had a lapse in coverage since July 6, 2012 (when the act was signed into law), not be resold, and not suffer repetitive losses.

Certain structures, however, would see much higher increases. Particularly hard hit are structures that are outside the high-risk areas of the 2007 map but will be inside the high-risk areas of the updated map. Approximately 28,800 one- to four-family structures fall into this category. A $429 annual premium on a structure previously outside the high-risk zones could well rise to $5,000 to $10,000 for the same amount of coverage if it is inside the high-risk area.

It is important to note that we have not been able to determine how frequently these scenarios will occur in practice. The key factor that precludes such an analysis is the lack of data on structure elevation relative to base flood elevation. However, the cases present plausible examples of how premiums could change with the adoption of the new map and the phase-out of subsidies.

Differences in Effects Among Residents

We examined differences in the effect that rate increases could have on families who own their own homes, as well as on renters and landlords.

Homeowners

Cost increases of this size would pose economic hardships for many households in the city. About 37 percent of households living in owner-occupied units in the floodplain earn less than $75,000 per year.[2] A $5,000 premium would amount to 6.6 percent of a $75,000 annual income. (For comparison, national census data show that, on average, households in owner-occupied housing units spend 1.8 percent of their annual pre-tax income on home insurance, maintenance, repair, and other housing expenses, excluding mortgage payments and property taxes.)

The value of owner-occupied homes in the high-risk areas would also likely decline. Given the magnitude of the premium increases, the reductions could be considerable. Previous research on housing prices in other regions of the country found that, under reasonable assumptions, a $500 increase in insurance premiums could be associated with a $10,000 decrease in property value. Further analysis is necessary to determine whether the effect might be different in New York City.

These consequences could make it impossible for some homeowners to stay in their homes. Many residents may have to move out of high-risk areas. Foreclosures

---

[2] For comparison, note that New York City defines *low-income households* as households with incomes less than or equal to 80 percent of area median income (AMI). The low-income threshold in New York City is $48,100 for a one-person household and $68,700 for a four-person household.

and short sales could increase. In some neighborhoods, homes could be vacant for some period of time. Lower property values would also affect city tax revenue, absent changes in tax rates.

Renters and Landlords

Renters account for approximately two-thirds of the households living in the high-risk areas of the new floodplain, with a large fraction living in multifamily and mixed-use dwellings. For them, the new premium increases might not create short-term hardships in the form of increased rents: The supply of housing units is fixed in the short term, and one would not expect the demand for rental housing in the high-risk areas to shift as a result of premium increases faced by landlords.

Although further work is needed to better understand the longer-term effects, several outcomes are possible. Under some scenarios, the major adjustment might be a decline in the land value for rental properties in the high-risk areas, analogous to the expectation for owner-occupied housing units. In that case, there would be little change in rents, even over the long run. Under other scenarios, the increase in flood insurance premiums could eventually reduce the rental housing stock and increase rents. Part of the calculation in all rental situations would be the effect of rent-control and stabilization policies in New York and how these policies would change over time.

Policy Options to Consider in Response to Premium Increases

New York City is considering a range of options that could provide residents with some relief in the cost of their insurance premiums, as summarized below. But better data are needed on household incomes and types of structures before developing a full range of potential responses.

Risk Mitigation

The most obvious way to reduce risk-based insurance premiums is to mitigate risk. This can be done on many levels—from developing dunes and integrated flood protection systems in order to reduce flooding to retrofitting buildings (by elevating a structure or its electrical equipment, for example) to reduce loss and facilitate quicker recovery in the event that flooding does occur.

Some of these measures, which have been applied elsewhere, would pose challenges in New York City because of the particular characteristics of the building stock in the city. For example, an initial analysis by the New York City Mayor's Office found that 39 percent of buildings (approximately 26,300) in the high-risk zones of the new floodplain would be difficult to elevate because they are on narrow lots or are attached or semi-attached buildings. It is therefore important to continue to search for innovative ways to reduce flood risk that are tailored to a dense urban environment like New York City.

Consequently, we recommend that policymakers take the following steps to identify the best risk-mitigation strategies:

- **Work with FEMA to collect data on structure elevations and other structure characteristics in the high-risk zones.** The key piece of missing information is structure elevation. We have developed plausible scenarios for these elevations, but more information on their distribution across the high-risk areas is needed. Besides facilitating better projections of flood insurance premiums, this information would allow better estimates of the benefits of coastal protection projects, as well as better decisions on what types of building-level mitigation measures would be appropriate.
- **Work with FEMA to make sure that the benefits of risk-mitigation measures are properly reflected in NFIP rates.** Much is to be gained from establishing a schedule of premium reductions for different structure types and risk-mitigation measures and making the information readily available to property owners.
- **Consider a multilayered approach to mitigation and protection.** A suite of mitigation tools and incentives should be considered based on specific physical and socioeconomic attributes of New York City neighborhoods. These might include low-interest loans or grants to individuals to fund mitigation efforts or larger-scale coastal protection measures to fortify whole neighborhoods. They might also include changes in land use that remove structures from some areas when property owners are willing to sell.
- **Work with FEMA and the New York State Department of Financial Services to increase the take-up rate.** Higher take-up rates mean that more resources are available for recovery after an event, but higher flood insurance premiums will put downward pressure on the already-moderate take-up rates. Efforts to increase the understanding of flood risk, as well as better enforcement of the mandatory purchase requirement, should be considered.

Affordability

Our analysis has used data on the income distribution in high-risk areas of the new flood maps as a whole. But premium levels and household income vary considerably across the floodplain. Better data are needed on the household incomes of people living in the structures facing the highest increases in insurance premiums. Such information will improve the understanding of the scope of the financial challenges for specific households and identify the number of households that would qualify for various types of assistance.

With a better understanding of the finances and structures of individual households, policymakers will be able to identify the best approaches to making insurance premiums more affordable. Examples of strategies that have been proposed include the following:

- **Provide assistance based on financial need.** The assistance could take several forms, including tax credits, grants, and vouchers that could be applied toward the cost of flood insurance. A major concern about such an approach, however, is that it would distort the price signal that motivates property owners to invest in risk-mitigation measures in order to reduce premiums. To address this concern, proposals have been made to couple a means-tested voucher program with a loan program, thereby implementing mitigation measures that make sense for the property.
- **Allow higher deductibles and establish a public program to share costs when flooding occurs.** The higher deductibles would mean lower premiums, and a deductible-sharing program funded by the public would cover part of a large deductible when an event occurs. Again, the effects on risk-mitigation incentives and actual mitigation would need to be considered.

Congress recognized the challenge of affordability that would be imposed by BW-12 and required that the NFIP study "methods of establishing an affordability framework" and that the National Academy of Sciences conduct an analysis of a means-tested voucher program. At the time of this writing, the National Academy of Sciences is about to begin the study, with phase 1 set for completion in late 2014.

In Conclusion

The threats posed by extreme weather are persistent, and it is only a matter of time before the next major storm strikes the eastern seaboard. But New York City can improve its resilience and speed its recovery by taking steps to mitigate the risk of flood damage and to increase flood insurance coverage for its residents and businesses. To achieve these goals, the city needs to work with FEMA and other agencies to collect better data on its coastal residents and the structures in which they live and work. It also needs to conduct further analysis to determine what packages of mitigation and affordability programs make sense for the city given its population and building typology. By taking such steps, New York City could become a leader in community resilience and a beacon for other coastal regions around the country.

Acknowledgments

Many thanks are due to the staff in the New York City Mayor's Office of Long-Term Planning and Sustainability for facilitating access to the city-level and Federal Emergency Management Agency (FEMA) data needed for the analysis and for identifying the key issues that should be addressed by the study. In particular, we would like to acknowledge the contributions of Leah Cohen, Katherine Greig, Sergej Mahnovski, Erika Lindsey, Basilia Yao, Daniel A. Zarrilli, Carrie Grassi, John H. Lee, Howard Slatkin, James P. Colgate, Joseph Ackroyd, Laura Smith, and Rebecca Kagan. Helpful background on the New York City building stock was provided by Thaddeus Pawlowski in the New York City Department of City Planning and the Office of Housing Recovery Operations, and David Gorman of the New York City Department of Finance aided in understanding the various New York City databases.

The authors would like to thank FEMA for providing data on the National Flood Insurance Program (NFIP) policies in New York City and claims related to Hurricane Sandy. We also benefited from discussions with FEMA Region 2 (Timothy P. Crowley), FEMA's New York City coastal remapping contractor (J. Andrew Martin of Dewberry), and FEMA actuaries (Thomas Hayes and Andy Neal). We also greatly appreciate the collaborative approach of David L. Miller and Roy E. Wright, as well as the coordinating efforts of Thomas Glen.

We are also indebted to Jean Marie Cho of the New York State Department of Financial Services for providing claims and market share statistics and to Jason Rutter of CoreLogic for providing data on the properties with mortgages in the high-risk areas of New York City. Jim Macdonald, adjunct RAND staff member, provided expertise on common coverages and exclusions in insurance policies.

The following insurance industry practitioners were very helpful in providing background on the insurance market in New York City and on their experiences with clients affected by Hurricane Sandy: Ian Macartney and Patrice Collingwood of Marsh; Ben Davidson of A. J. Gallagher; Thomas Becker of Wells Fargo Insurance Services; Scott Gunter of Chubb Commercial Insurance; Roger Odle, John Manarra, Edward Collins, and Sean Meehan of Allstate; Christopher H. Perini of Verisk Analytics; Martin Koles of M. Koles and Associates; Danielle McHeffey and Kirsten Squires of Maran Corporate Risk Associates; Robert P. Hartwig of the Insurance Industry

Institute; and Patricia A. Borowski of the National Association of Professional Insurance Agents. We are also thankful for the insights of J. Robert Hunter of the Consumer Federation of America.

Constructive peer reviews of draft reports were provided by Steven Garber and Craig A. Bond at RAND and Carolyn Kousky of Resources for the Future. We thank them for providing insightful comments on very compressed timelines. At RAND, Debra Knopman and Paul Heaton provided helpful guidance throughout the project, and Tom LaTourrette coordinated the review process. We would also like to thank Lisa Bernard for skillful editing and Jocelyn Lofstrom for coordinating the publication process.

Abbreviations

ABFE	Advisory Base Flood Elevation
ACS	American Community Survey
ADCIRC	ADvanced CIRCulation
ALE	additional living expense
BFE	Base Flood Elevation
BW-12	Biggert-Waters Flood Insurance Reform Act of 2012
CBRA	Coastal Barrier Resources Act
CCO	consultation coordination officer
CIAB	Council of Insurance Agents and Brokers
C-MAP	Coastal Market Assistance Program
CPP	commercial package policy
EC	elevation certificate
EE	eligibility extension
Fannie Mae	Federal National Mortgage Association
FEMA	Federal Emergency Management Agency
FIRM	flood insurance rate map
Freddie Mac	Federal Home Loan Mortgage Corporation
GAO	U.S. Government Accountability Office
GIS	geographic information system
IIABNY	Independent Insurance Agents and Brokers of New York

LFD	letter of final determination
MPR	mandatory purchase requirement
NFIP	National Flood Insurance Program
NWS	National Weather Service
NYPIUA	New York Property Insurance Underwriting Association
OLTPS	Office of Long-Term Planning and Sustainability
PRP	Preferred Risk Policy
PWM	Preliminary Work Map
RAMPP	Risk Assessment, Mapping, and Planning Partners
RCBAP	Residential Condominium Building Association Policy
Risk MAP	Risk Mapping, Assessment, and Planning
RMS	Risk Management Solutions
SFHA	special flood hazard area
SWAN	Simulating WAves Nearshore
SWEL	stillwater elevation
WHAFIS	Wave Height Analysis for Flood Insurance Studies

CHAPTER ONE

Introduction

As New York City's coastal residents and businesses struggle to recover from one of the most destructive storms in U.S. history, they are also confronting changes in the flood insurance landscape that will pose other challenges in the future. These changes include revisions to the flood map drawn by the Federal Emergency Management Agency (FEMA) that defines areas at greatest risk of flooding during a storm, and reforms to the government-backed National Flood Insurance Program (NFIP), which has been operating at a loss in recent years. These developments will provide a more accurate basis for assessing flood risk and setting premiums that reflect those risks. But they will also impose financial burdens on the very people who are reeling from the destruction of their homes and businesses in the path of Hurricane Sandy.[1]

The storm itself was devastating, flooding land in all five boroughs of the city when it hit on October 29, 2012. The storm surge reached nearly 88,700 buildings, more than 300,000 housing units, and 23,400 businesses,[2] many of which are old residential structures that had not been built to modern standards and were either uninsured or underinsured for flood damage. Because homeowner's insurance typically excludes coverage for damage caused by floods and affordable flood insurance has historically been difficult to find from private insurers, the federal government established the NFIP in 1968. This insurance is available to all property owners, renters, and businesses in communities that join the NFIP, but it is mandated for any structure located in a high-risk area (the 100-year floodplain) that has a federally backed mortgage on the property. Hurricane Sandy, however, exposed the fact that a modest proportion of residential units in the storm path carried such policies.

FEMA's updated flood map will increase the number of households required to buy flood insurance. This update, combined with recent legislative changes to the NFIP that reduce the subsidies in the program and make the rates more actuarially

---

[1] We refer to the storm as *Hurricane Sandy* throughout the report because that is a common reference to the event, although it is sometimes referred to as *Superstorm Sandy*. The storm was declared a hurricane on October 24, 2012, by the National Weather Service but was downgraded to a post–tropical cyclone on October 29, 2012, shortly before making landfall in New York and New Jersey.

[2] City of New York, "A Stronger, More Resilient New York," June 2013.

sound, will make that insurance more expensive. As is described later in this report, the current flood map of all coastal areas, including the New York City area, is based on modeling and data that are 30 years old. The new coastal storm study and remapping of the New York City area were well under way at the time Hurricane Sandy hit. The newly defined floodplains use the latest storm-surge and wave models that include vast amounts of information about the behavior of storms in any given area, as well as wave setup (the increase in water level), wave heights, and the wave run-up (the vertical height of waves crashing against a beach or structure).

In January and February 2013, FEMA released the new Advisory Base Flood Elevation (ABFE) map for New York City so property owners could rebuild based on this updated information, but it approximated flood risk information. In June 2013, that map was then superseded by the Preliminary Work Map (PWM) that incorporated more-refined wave modeling. The PWM indicates that New York City's floodplain has expanded significantly to include about 32,000 additional structures in the 100-year floodplain. This essentially doubles the number of structures in the high-risk flood zones. In addition, Base Flood Elevations (BFEs) for structures in the flood zones are increasing more than 2 feet on average and more than 5 feet in some cases.[3] Per New York City building codes, new construction in the floodplain must be elevated to BFE plus "freeboard" (which is 2 feet for single-family homes) or else flood-proofed (physical efforts to mitigate flood damage). In accordance with NFIP regulations, New York City requires that a damaged structure be rebuilt to current building-code standards if the repair cost is greater than 50 percent of its market value.

Besides these developments, Congress has also authorized FEMA to make changes to the NFIP that will eliminate artificially low rates and will base premiums on the full risk of flood damage. The goal of these changes is to make the NFIP more financially solvent and reduce the amount the program borrows from the Treasury. Grandfathering, which was put into place to reduce the financial impact of a new map, will also be eliminated: Instead of allowing a property that is being mapped into a higher-risk zone or higher flood elevation to keep its earlier designation (and premium rates), the new provisions require FEMA to increase the premiums of buildings affected by these map changes by 20 percent per year over five years, at which point they will reach FEMA's assessment of the full-risk rate. Another provision of the reforms will incent banks to be more vigorous in enforcing the flood insurance mandate for structures with federally backed mortgages.

Taken together, these changes in the flood insurance market could put many residents along New York City's vulnerable coastline at risk of losing their homes if they cannot afford the mandated insurance policies. Hardest hit will be low- to moderate-

---

[3]   BFE is expressed in feet above a reference sea level. So, for example, a typical BFE in New York City might be 12 or 14 feet. Increases in BFE are examined in Chapter Four.

income residents, including communities of working-class families who have lived on or near the coast for generations.

The critical policy issue for city leaders is how to provide coastal residents with flood insurance that is based soundly on risk but is not priced beyond what residents can reasonably be expected to pay. A related issue is how to encourage residents and businesses in high-risk areas to purchase flood insurance and take steps to mitigate flood risk that will also lower their premiums.

Study Purpose

As a government, New York City is concerned with ensuring that its residents and their property are safe. When events like Hurricane Sandy hit and residents incur damages, the benefits of having insurance and, in this case, flood insurance are that rebuilding and recovery are affordable and can begin sooner than without insurance. This report provides the most-comprehensive analysis to date on flood insurance take-up in New York City and begins the discussion of the information needed to develop and assess various policy options aimed at mitigating risk and making insurance premiums more affordable. It is intended to provide information to the New York City Mayor's Office of Long-Term Planning and Sustainability (OLTPS), which commissioned this research, and federal, state, and other local policymakers who are dedicated to increasing the city's resilience to flooding.

We begin by describing the setting prior to Hurricane Sandy: the number and characteristics of structures in the floodplain, the take-up rates for flood insurance, and the typical flood insurance premiums and coverage limits. We then describe insurance payments following the storm, gaps in coverage that became evident during Hurricane Sandy, and the storm's effects on general insurance market conditions and insurance rates in New York City.

Against this backdrop, we offer detailed descriptions of how the new flood map and the changes to the NFIP are likely to affect residents and businesses: specifically, how many structures and households are included in the expanded floodplain; the characteristics of those residents, households, and housing units; and examples of possible changes in their flood insurance premiums. Finally, we describe some of the data and information New York City will need in order to develop and assess various policy options to address the affordability of flood insurance. Appendixes provide background on the NFIP, the private flood insurance market, and assumptions and calculations that underlie the analysis.

Our Approach

The difficulty of conducting research on insurance markets is acquiring the relevant data, especially with limited time. We collected as much quantitative data as we could; where such data were not available, we relied on interviews and published reports from the insurance industry. In this section, we provide a high-level overview of our methods. More detail is provided in the following chapters.

To describe the status of the residential flood insurance market just before Hurricane Sandy, we collected data on NFIP policies in force at the individual policy level, which allowed us to assess take-up rates for flood insurance. The NFIP also provided information on damage claims for New York City after Hurricane Sandy as of February 2013. To estimate insured losses, we drew on data collected by the insurance industry.

To describe the structures and residents at risk in current and future flood zones, we used geospatial (geographic information system [GIS]) parcel-level data that describe the structures on each parcel, whether there is a mortgage on the parcel, the NFIP flood zone, and other information, including type of business or type of residential structure. To evaluate take-up rates for flood insurance, we used these GIS parcel data and overlaid NFIP data on active policies. We used data on mortgages to describe levels of compliance with the mandatory purchase requirement (MPR) for flood insurance. We conducted this analysis for both the current flood map and the new PWM to identify how many more people, homes, and businesses will be affected when the new flood map and the elimination of NFIP subsidies become effective.

To analyze the sociodemographic characteristics of the affected population, we drew on the most-recent census data available, the 2006–2010 American Community Survey (ACS) five-year estimates. We report data at the smallest geographic level at which key demographics (e.g., income, demographics, housing data) are publicly available—typically either the census block group or census tract. The five-year estimates represent the average characteristics of households in a given census block group in 2006–2010. Because these data are multiyear estimates rather than point-in-time estimates, they do not capture any rapid changes that might be occurring in neighborhood characteristics.[4]

It was more difficult to collect quantitative data on the private insurance market from private insurers during the study period. To help fill this gap, we conducted interviews with 11 insurance agents and brokers who represent New York City property owners, both residential and commercial. These agents and brokers represent residential clients in the standard and high-end markets and commercial clients from small, middle-market, and large commercial firms. We also conducted six additional inter-

---

[4]   U.S. Census Bureau, American Community Survey, 2009.

views with other insurance industry officials, insurance regulators, FEMA, consumer advocates, and mapping and data experts.

To examine the implications of the new PWM and NFIP reforms for the price of flood insurance, we relied on insurance industry reports and our interviews. We conclude the report by discussing some of the data and information New York City will need in order to develop and assess various policy options, as well as solutions to consider, to make flood insurance affordable for residents and businesses.

CHAPTER TWO

The Setting Prior to Hurricane Sandy

This chapter discusses the number of structures in New York City in different building classes, the number of structures in high-risk flood zones, and the take-up rate for flood insurance for both residences and businesses on the eve of Hurricane Sandy. It also examines the typical prices of flood insurance in New York City pre–Hurricane Sandy.

Overview of the Areas Mapped as High Risk in New York City When Hurricane Sandy Hit

FEMA issues a map that identifies areas of flood risk across the country. The first flood insurance rate map (FIRM) issued for New York City became effective on November 16, 1983. Additional revised FIRMs were issued in February 1991, May 1992, July 1994, May 2001, and September 2007 that revised certain riverine areas, but the coastal modeling was not updated.[1] As a result, the FIRM in effect on the eve of Hurricane Sandy, and the FIRM that is still officially in place, is based on coastal modeling and data that are 30 years old.

A map of the high-risk areas of the 2007 FIRM is provided in Figure 2.1. The high-risk areas are those marked as A or V zones and correspond to those areas that have a 1-percent chance of flooding in any given year (also known as the 100-year floodplain). V zones are areas at risk of experiencing waves greater than 3 feet in height. NFIP premiums are higher and building-code requirements more stringent in V zones than in A zones (see Appendix A for a description of the flood zone designations). Approximately 10 percent of the land area in the high-risk areas is in V zones, with the remainder in A zones.[2]

---

[1] FEMA, "Community Status Book Report: Nation—Communities Participating in the National Flood Program," October 10, 2013f; referenced April 23, 2013. The riverine areas account for approximately 8 percent of the high-risk area of the 2007 FIRM (2.7 square miles out of 33 square miles). The remainder are areas subject to coastal flooding (Erika Lindsey, Policy Analyst, New York City Mayor's Office of Long-Term Planning and Sustainability, personal communication, September 10, 2013).

[2] Erika Lindsey, New York City Mayor's Office of Long-Term Planning and Sustainability, personal communication, October 15, 2013.

Figure 2.1
High-Risk Areas of the 2007 Flood Insurance Rate Map

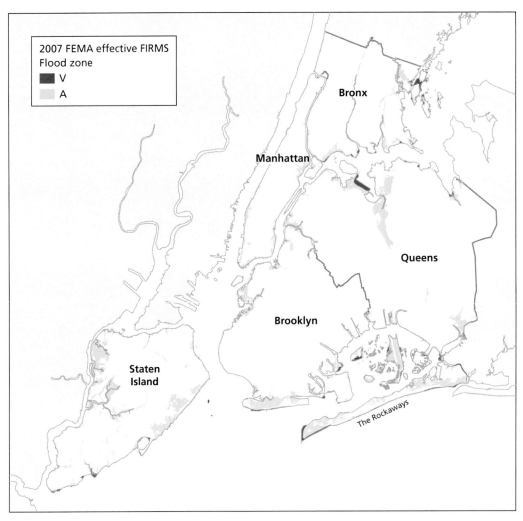

SOURCES: FEMA Map Service Center data for 2007.
RAND RR328-2.1

Table 2.1 provides an overview of the property parcels, structures, and housing in the areas mapped as high risk in the 2007 FIRM. Parcel data, often referred to in New York City as tax lots, were provided by the New York City Department of City Planning. As can be seen in Table 2.1, there are approximately 35,700 structures on 31,900 parcels in the high-risk area of the 2007 FIRM. Also shown is the number of housing units according to Department of City Planning data. Although the majority of structures are associated with one- to four-family dwellings, most residential housing units are in multifamily structures or mixed commercial and residential properties. Even in densely populated New York City, roughly 60 percent of the parcels and

Table 2.1
Number of Parcels, Structures, and Housing Units in High-Risk Areas of the 2007 Flood Insurance Rate Map

Structure Type	Parcels	Structures	Housing Units
Residential	21,000	29,200	161,600
One- to four-family dwelling	19,100	25,800	31,400
Single-family	12,000	17,500	15,700
Two-family	5,800	6,600	11,500
Three- and four-family	1,400	1,700	4,300
Condominium	100	700	2,500
Multifamily dwelling	800	1,400	86,000
Mixed-use dwelling	1,000	1,300	41,600
Commercial	3,500	4,300	500
Commercial and industrial	2,000	2,700	400
Transportation and utility	1,500	1,600	10
Condominium	20	30	0
Other	6,700	1,800	500
Missing information on parcel type	700	400	200
Total	31,900	35,700	162,700

SOURCE: New York City parcel data.

NOTE: RAND's building-count methodology differed slightly from that used by the city in its report *A Stronger, More Resilient New York*. As a result, building counts in the two reports differ slightly. Because of rounding, rows might not sum precisely. Numbers have been rounded to the nearest hundred (numbers smaller than 100, to the nearest ten).

72 percent of the structures in the 100-year floodplain are associated with one- to four-family dwellings.

To get a better sense of the differences between the various types of residential structures, we viewed a random sample of condominiums, multifamily dwellings, and mixed-use dwellings in all five boroughs using Google Earth. Condominiums tended to be small to medium-sized buildings with multiple units. Mixed-use, residential dwellings appeared as one would expect, with shops on the bottom floor and residential units above. The multifamily-dwelling category had the least amount of consistency. Some of these properties were small to medium-sized buildings with multiple units, but we also found several examples of large residential buildings with commercial space on the ground floor. These buildings might more accurately be categorized as mixed-use, residential buildings.

As is evident from Table 2.1, there can be multiple structures on the same parcel. For example, the data show that there are sometimes two structures on parcels with single-family homes (see Table 2.2). The second structure on many of these parcels might be a detached garage—which would not require a separate NFIP policy if used only as a garage. But if this garage also has an office or rental unit, then a second NFIP policy would be required. Occasionally, there are a large number of structures on some parcels. For example, the Breezy Point cooperative in Queens is one property parcel that is classified as single-family homes. However, the Breezy Point parcel includes 1,897 structures and 1,885 residential units, each of which is a single-family home. Even though some parcels have a large number of structures, 66 percent of one- to four-family structures are on parcels with one structure.

For comparison, Table 2.3 shows the number of parcels, structures, and residential units in New York City overall. Approximately 4 percent of the parcels, 4 percent of the structures, and 5 percent of the residential units in New York City are in the high-risk areas of the 2007 FIRM.

As expected, a high percentage of structures in New York City's high-risk areas were built before the first FIRM was issued for New York City in November 1983. The

Table 2.2
Number of Structures on Parcels Classified as One- to Four-Family Dwellings in High-Risk Areas of 2007 Flood Insurance Rate Map

Number of Structures	Number of Parcels	
	Single-Family	Two- to Four-Family
0	10	8
1	10,760	6,117
2	1,148	898
3	29	57
4	11	16
5–10	7	13
11–50	7	1
51–100	7	0
100–1,897	4	0
Total	11,983	7,110

SOURCE: New York City parcel data.

Table 2.3
Number of Parcels, Structures, and Housing Units in New York City

Structure Type	Parcels		Structures		Housing Units	
	Number	Percentage in High-Risk Areas of 2007 FIRM	Number	Percentage in High-Risk Areas of 2007 FIRM	Number	Percentage in High-Risk Areas of 2007 FIRM
Residential	753,400	2.8	913,500	3.2	3,391,500	4.8
One- to four-family dwelling	652,700	2.9	779,700	3.3	1,098,800	2.9
Condominium	2,900	3.7	12,500	5.8	63,700	4.0
Multifamily dwelling	49,300	1.6	64,700	2.2	1,600,700	5.4
Mixed-use dwelling	48,500	2.0	56,600	2.2	628,300	6.6
Commercial	54,600	6.4	58,500	7.4	9,600	4.8
Commercial and industrial	36,200	5.5	42,200	6.4	9,300	4.9
Transportation and utility	18,100	8.2	16,000	10.1	300	2.0
Condominium	300	7.7	300	8.6	0	—
Other	46,500	14.4	19,000	9.6	23,600	2.0
Missing	4,600	16.4	1,900	19.7	200	88.4
Total	859,000	3.7	992,900	3.6	3,424,800	4.7

SOURCE: New York City parcel data. Because of rounding, rows might not sum precisely. Counts have been rounded to the nearest hundred (numbers smaller than 100, to the nearest ten).

NFIP refers to these structures as *pre-FIRM*.[3] Eighty percent of structures and 78 percent of one- to four-family structures in the high-risk areas of the 2007 FIRM were
constructed prior to November 1983 (see Table 2.4). However, only about one-quarter
of residential condominium parcels are pre-FIRM, indicating that most condominiums were built more recently, though there are not a large number of condominiums
in the high-risk flood zones.

Take-Up Rates for Flood Insurance in High-Risk Areas on the Eve of Hurricane Sandy

In this section, we examine the proportion of structures with flood insurance compared
with the proportion without, on the eve of Hurricane Sandy in the high-risk areas of
New York City. The share of the total number of structures with flood insurance is also
referred to as the *take-up rate*. We first discuss residential structures and then turn to

Table 2.4
Structures in High-Risk Areas of 2007 Flood Insurance Rate Map Built Before the FIRM

Structure Type	Number of Pre-FIRM Structures	Percentage of All Structures in Structure-Type Category
Residential		
One- to four-family dwelling	20,100	78
Condominium	400	55
Multifamily dwelling	1,300	90
Mixed-use dwelling	1,000	80
Commercial		
Commercial and industrial	2,300	85
Transportation and utility	1,500	92
Condominium	20	77
Other	1,700	92
Missing	300	92
All structures	28,600	80

SOURCE: New York City parcel data.

NOTE: Because of rounding, rows might not sum precisely. Numbers have been rounded to the nearest
hundred (numbers smaller than 100, to the nearest ten).

---

[3] *Pre-FIRM* is used in this report to denote when a structure was built, not whether it receives a subsidized rate
from the NFIP.

commercial structures. For residential structures, we also examine the percentage of these structures subject to the NFIP MPR and the percentage that comply with the requirement.

Residential Flood Insurance Take-Up Rates

The NFIP is the predominant provider of flood insurance for one- to four-family dwellings and can be an important source of insurance for other residential properties. As explained in Appendix A, federal law directs federally regulated lenders to require flood insurance on properties in high-risk zones that are used as collateral (an overview of the NFIP and the coverage offered is included in Appendix A).[4] Loans on such properties that are sold to government-sponsored enterprises, such as the Federal National Mortgage Association (Fannie Mae) and the Federal Home Loan Mortgage Corporation (Freddie Mac) are also subject to the requirement. In this section, we investigate the take-up rate for NFIP policies, as well as compliance with the MPR.

To do so, we plotted the location of each NFIP policy in place as of October 31, 2012, on property parcel maps for New York City. The NFIP policy data provided to us by FEMA contained the latitude and longitude of the structure covered by each policy. The 25,916 NFIP policies in New York City were plotted onto a map of 858,968 parcels. In most cases, the policies lined up neatly with the parcels; however, in about 10 percent of the cases, the policy coordinates fell in the middle of the street or otherwise outside a parcel. In such cases, standard GIS algorithms were used to assign the policy to the nearest parcel.

To determine whether NFIP policies were accurately assigned to parcels, we compared the building address on the NFIP policy with the address of the parcel to which the policy was assigned. We randomly sampled 491 of the 25,916 NFIP policies in New York City as of October 31, 2012 (1.9 percent). For residential parcels, the address on the NFIP policy matched the parcel address in 88 percent of the cases.

Take-Up Rate for One- to Four-Family Structures

Table 2.5 presents the take-up rate for one- to four-family structures in the high-risk areas of the 2007 FIRM. We focus on one- to four-family structures because they account for 88 percent of residential structures in the high-risk areas (see Table 2.1). In addition, flood insurance for mixed-use and multifamily dwellings is often purchased in the private sector, so NFIP figures provide only a partial picture of the flood insurance in place on these types of structures.

Because, as discussed above, garages can be covered by the NFIP policy on the main structure, we base our estimate of the take-up rate for one- to four-family structures on parcels with one structure (which amount to 66 percent of the structures on

---

[4]   The property owner can purchase flood insurance from the NFIP or comparable coverage from a private insurer.

Table 2.5
Take-Up of National Flood Insurance Program Policies for One- to Four-Family Structures in the High-Risk Zones of the 2007 Flood Insurance Rate Map on One- to Four-Family Structures (as of October 31, 2012)

Measure	Estimate
Take-up rate (percentage of structures with NFIP policy) (based on 16,877 parcels)[a]	55
Lower bound for take-up rate (based on 19,093 parcels)	49
Upper bound for take-up rate (based on 19,093 parcels)	60

SOURCE: Merge of NFIP policy file with New York City parcel data.

[a] Based on parcels with one structure.

one- to four-family parcels). We do this to avoid the uncertainty over whether one NFIP policy covers all the structures on the parcel (as would be the case for a home with a garage that is used solely as a garage) or whether a separate policy is needed for each structure on the parcel. The take-up rate is calculated by dividing the number of such parcels with at least one NFIP policy that provides building coverage by the number of parcels.

As can be seen in the table, 55 percent of these structures have building coverage provided by the NFIP. To examine sensitivity of the results to assumptions about whether a separate NFIP policy is required on each structure on the one- to four-family parcels, we constructed lower and upper bounds for the take-up rate. In the lower bound, it is assumed that each structure requires a separate NFIP policy, which would not be the case, for example, when a structure on a parcel is used solely as a garage. In the upper bound, it is assumed that the (often multiple) NFIP policies on a parcel cover every structure on that parcel. That would not be the case at Breezy Point, for example, where the number of NFIP policies is far smaller than the number of structures on the parcel (1,897). The 55-percent take-up rate estimate lies approximately in the middle of the 49- to 60-percent range spanned by the lower and upper bounds.

In a previous RAND study, take-up rates for single-family homes in high-risk flood zones was estimated at 49 percent nationally as of 2005, with a 95-percent statistical confidence interval of 42 to 57 percent.[5] The rate varied considerably by region, with the take-up for homes in high-risk flood zones in the Northeast at 28 percent (95-percent confidence interval of 11 to 46 percent). New York City, however, was excluded from that analysis. The 55-percent take-up rate found here for New York City

---

[5]   Lloyd Dixon, Noreen Clancy, Seth A. Seabury, and Adrian Overton, *The National Flood Insurance Program's Market Penetration Rate: Estimates and Policy Implications*, Santa Monica, Calif.: RAND Corporation, TR-300-FEMA, 2006.

lies within the 95-percent confidence interval for the national average found in the previous study.

Banks have the authority to "force-place" flood insurance on homes in high-risk flood zones with mortgages that do not have flood insurance.[6] They typically force-place private flood insurance policies, not NFIP policies, so the percentage of homes with flood policies will be somewhat higher than that indicated in Table 2.5.[7] Dixon, Clancy, Bender, et al. found that lender-placed flood insurance policies amount to about 3 percent of NFIP policies nationally.[8] Adjusting the estimate for one- to four-family homes in Table 2.5 to account for lender-placed policies increases the structure take-up rate to 57 percent.

Compliance with the Mandatory Purchase Requirement

To determine which properties in New York City are likely subject to the MPR, we acquired data on the mortgages in place on New York City parcels. We provided a list of parcels, including address and parcel number, in the high-risk areas of the 2007 FIRM and in the high-risk areas of the revised flood map (see Chapter Four) to CoreLogic, a company that consolidates property and mortgage information from various sources. If CoreLogic was able to identify the parcel in its database, it indicated whether or not there was a mortgage in place on the parcel and provided several pieces of information about the mortgage, including initial mortgage amount and inception date. We then investigated the take-up rate for parcels with and without mortgages.

The results of the analysis are shown in Table 2.6. Again, the calculations are based on one- to four-family parcels with one structure. According to the CoreLogic data, 77 percent of one- to four-family homes in the high-risk areas of the 2007 FIRM have mortgages. Census data (presented in Table 5.1 in Chapter Five) show that 62 percent of owner-occupied housing units in the high-risk areas of the 2007 FIRM have mortgages, substantially below the 77-percent figure. The two figures are not necessarily inconsistent, however, because the CoreLogic data include properties that are not owner-occupied. Nevertheless, the reasons for the discrepancy need to be further examined.

As shown in Table 2.6, 65 percent of one- to four-family structures in the high-risk areas with mortgages have NFIP building coverage. This finding is consistent with previous estimates for the nation as a whole. Dixon, Clancy, Seabury, et al. found that,

---

[6]   Lenders are required to purchase flood insurance on a property subject to the MPR if the property owner fails to do so.

[7]   Lloyd Dixon, Noreen Clancy, Bruce Bender, and Patricia K. Ehrler, *The Lender-Placed Flood Insurance Market for Residential Properties*, Santa Monica, Calif.: RAND Corporation, TR-468-FEMA, 2007.

[8]   Dixon, Clancy, Bender, et al., 2007.

Table 2.6
Take-Up of National Flood Insurance Program Policies for One- to Four-Family Structures in the High-Risk Zones of the 2007 Flood Insurance Rate Map, by Mortgage Status (as of October 31, 2012)

Measure	Estimate
Percentage of structures with mortgages (based on 16,743 parcels)	77
Take-up rate for structures with mortgages (based on 12,974 parcels)	65
Take-up rate for structures without mortgages (based on 3,769 parcels)	21

SOURCE: Merging of CoreLogic, NFIP policy-in-force, and New York City parcel data.

NOTE: Based on one- to four-family parcels with one structure.

nationwide, 67 percent of single-family homes that were likely to have a mortgage also had an NFIP policy (95-confidence interval 59 to 75).[9]

To estimate compliance with the MPR, the incidence of loans with non–federally regulated lenders (which are not subject to the MPR) would need to be considered. Estimates of the percentage of home mortgages nationwide that are provided by federally regulated lenders are in the 85- to 90-percent range, so including this factor would likely increase the compliance rate from the percentage found here, but not by a great deal.[10] Including force-placed policies, as was discussed earlier, would also increase the estimated compliance rate, but not by much.

Although those we interviewed from the insurance industry believed that enforcement of the MPR was spotty in New York City before the financial crisis of 2008, there was a sense that enforcement had improved considerably as a result of the public and regulatory scrutiny of mortgage financing after the crisis. Several agents reported that a

---

[9]   Dixon, Clancy, Seabury, et al., 2006. To provide a check on the estimates, we also obtained information on mortgages from the New York City Department of Finance. The department was able to identify those parcels for which property taxes were paid by a mortgage service company, thus indicating that a mortgage was attached to the property. Mortgages may exist on other parcels but would not be flagged in the New York City data. These include properties with private mortgages, mortgages from small banks that receive a paper real estate bill, and properties that have a mortgage but the taxpayer pays the property tax directly to New York City. The New York City data thus show mortgages with escrowed taxes and are missing mortgages with unescrowed taxes. Precise data on the percentage of property owners with mortgages with unescrowed taxes are not readily available.

The Department of Finance data showed that 51 percent of the one- to four-family structures in the high-risk area of the 2007 FIRM had mortgages and that 71 percent of the structures with mortgages had NFIP structure coverage. The analysis was based on one- to four-family parcels with one structure. The similarity of the 71 percent to the 65-percent estimate based on the mortgage data from CoreLogic provides confidence that the share of homes in high-risk areas with mortgages that have flood insurance is roughly two-thirds.

[10]   See Dixon, Clancy, Seabury, et al. (2006) for discussion of the percentage of mortgages with federally regulated lenders.

home in a high-risk flood zone can no longer close a loan without flood insurance and that banks are much more consistent in requiring that flood insurance be maintained on existing loans. It was also noted that the low interest rates in the past few years have led to a significant increase in the refinancing of residential and commercial properties and that many properties that were out of compliance previously were likely brought into compliance during the refinancing process. The dramatically increased fines (from $350 to $2,000) under the Biggert-Waters Flood Insurance Reform Act of 2012 (BW-12) for lenders that have properties out of compliance may further increase compliance with the MPR over time.

Table 2.6 indicates that owners of one- to four-family structures will seldom buy flood insurance unless required to do so. The take-up rate is only 21 percent on one- to four-family parcels that do not have mortgages. This low take-up rate in the so-called voluntary flood insurance market is consistent with previous nationwide estimates.[11]

Commercial Flood Insurance Take-Up Rates

NFIP policies are not common on commercial structures. Only 19 percent of structures in the commercial and industrial subcategory in Table 2.1 carried NFIP building coverage prior to Hurricane Sandy. The rate was 9 percent for transportation and utility structures. Both figures refer to the high-risk zones of the 2007 FIRM.[12] However, commercial firms often buy flood coverage in the private market. (Appendix A discusses the private insurance market and the types of flood coverage available.)

Interviews with informed industry sources suggest that flood insurance take-up among large commercial firms is very high, estimated at 80–90 percent. These take-up rates apply regardless of whether insured structures are in or out of the high-risk areas. The high take-up rate is primarily because these firms tend to purchase inclusive manuscript policies in the private market. The large insured firms typically do not buy NFIP policies, except occasionally to reduce a high deductible on the manuscript policy (see Appendix A for more detail).

Take-up rates for the small firms at the other end of the market are thought to be very low—on the order of 5 to 10 percent. This view was shared by all the interviewees who commented on the topic. Interviewees were not able to clearly distinguish take-up rates inside versus outside of the high-risk zones for this class of firms, and this 5- to 10-percent range likely applies to all small businesses, regardless of location. However, the sense was the take-up rate was very low whether in or out of the high-risk areas.

---

[11] Dixon, Clancy, Seabury, et al. (2006, p. 30) found that take-up for single-family homes in high-risk flood zones nationwide that are not subject to the MPR is on the order of 20 percent.

[12] The method used to map NFIP policies onto parcels described in the "Residential Flood Insurance Take-Up Rates" section above was also applied to commercial parcels. The match rate for commercial parcels is lower than for residential properties, although the number of commercial parcels audited was small (18). NFIP take-up results for the commercial parcel types should be interpreted with care, and further work is needed to understand how they might change as the matching process is improved.

If they buy coverage at all, small firms rely in large measure on the NFIP for flood insurance.

Take-up rates for the middle market range between these two extremes; the smallest firms in the middle market have take-up rates similar to those of small firms. According to the interviews, the largest middle-market firms have take-up rates similar to those of large firms, although interviewees pointed out that there are not many of these large, middle-market firms. As discussed in Appendix A, $50,000 and $500,000 in annual premiums are reasonable cutoffs for the division between the small and middle and between the middle and large insurance markets, respectively. We have not been able to develop estimates of the percentage of structures in the high-risk flood zones of New York City that are owned by firms that fall into each of these categories.

National Flood Insurance Program Premiums and Policy Limits in New York City

This section describes annual flood insurance premiums in New York City as of October 2012 and the amount of coverage purchased. The analysis is based on the 25,916 residential and commercial NFIP policies in force in New York City as of October 31, 2012.[13] The findings provide a base against which to assess the changes in premiums due to the elimination of subsidies under BW-12 and flood-map changes. Breakdowns by structure type and flood zone are reported using the categories provided by the NFIP on the policy records. The four categories available for structure type are single-family residential, two- to four-family residential, other residential, and nonresidential.

As shown in Table 2.7, the average annual premium paid on single-family and two- to four-family structures is about $1,000, with higher premiums paid in the other residential and nonresidential categories. More-detailed information on the premiums paid on one- to four-family structures is included in Table 2.8. Note that the amount of coverage provided by these policies varies by policy. As expected, average rates in the high-risk zones for one- to four-family structures are higher than those in the lower-risk zones (see Table 2.8). Even though the rates on some pre-FIRM structures are subsidized, the average premium for pre-FIRM structures in the high-risk zones is nearly double that for post-FIRM structures in high-risk areas. This difference reflects the likelihood that many post-FIRM structures were constructed with higher elevations relative to the BFE than pre-FIRM structures.

Table 2.9 displays the number of NFIP policies by the amount of building coverage purchased (the policy limit for building coverage) for one- to four-family struc-

---

[13] This is the full set of policies in force. FEMA uses the term *contract* to refer to the flood insurance agreement on a particular structure or multiple structures. A structure can contain multiple housing units (e.g., a four-family structure), and FEMA refers to the number of housing units insured as the number of policies in force. There are currently approximately 4.5 million contracts and 5.5 million policies in force. In this report, we use *policies* to refer to FEMA contracts, unless otherwise indicated.

Table 2.7
Average Annual Premium for National Flood Insurance Program Policies in New York City (for policies in force as of October 31, 2012)

Structure Type	Number of Policies	Average Premium (dollars)	5th Percentile (dollars)	95th Percentile (dollars)
Single-family residential	16,118	1,023	274	2,523
Two- to four-family residential	6,299	1,038	276	2,595
Other residential	2,136	2,871	178	6,906
Nonresidential	1,363	3,811	517	9,613
Total	25,916	1,325	247	2,996

SOURCE: NFIP policy data.

Table 2.8
Average Annual Premium for National Flood Insurance Program Policies in New York City for One- to Four-Family Structures (for policies in force as of October 31, 2012)

Structure Location and Construction Date	Number	Average Premium (dollars)	5th Percentile (dollars)	95th Percentile (dollars)
In high-risk flood zone of 2007 FIRM	11,217	1,547	358	2,908
Pre-FIRM	8,034	1,784	515	2,777
Post-FIRM	3,183	949	340	2,980
Outside high-risk flood zone of 2007 FIRM	11,199	506	185	1,358
Pre-FIRM	8,779	486	185	1,327
Post-FIRM	2,420	577	236	1,502
All policies	22,416[a]	1,027	276	2,538

SOURCE: NFIP premium data.

[a] The construction date for one policy is missing, and the observation is omitted from this table.

tures. Nearly three-quarters of policies carry the $250,000 limit for one- to four-family structures.

Table 2.9
Building Coverage Limit for National Flood Insurance
Program Policies for One- to Four-Family Structures

Policy Limit for Building Coverage ($)	Number	Percentage
Pre-FIRM structures		
0 to 50,000	1,229	5
50,001 to 100,000	878	4
100,001 to 150,000	903	4
150,001 to 200,000	1,087	5
200,001 to 249,999	761	3
250,000	11,937	53
Post-FIRM structures		
0 to 50,000	270	1
50,001 to 100,000	113	1
100,001 to 150,000	198	1
150,001 to 200,000	265	1
200,001 to 249,999	284	1
250,000	4,455	20
Total	22,380	100

SOURCE: NFIP premium data. Uses flood zone and occupancy as recorded by the NFIP in its policy-in-force database.

NOTE: Because of rounding, percentages do not sum to 100. Thirty-six policies for one- to four-family homes recorded policy limits greater than $250,000. The maximum policy limit for a residential structure is $250,000, and these policies were omitted from the table. The 36 policies are conceivably condominium policies with two to four units. Also, the construction date of one policy is missing, and the observation is omitted from this table.

CHAPTER THREE

Insurance Payments After Hurricane Sandy and Hurricane Sandy's Impact on Insurance Markets

This chapter describes the insurance payments on claims related to Hurricane Sandy and provides an overview of the performance of the insurance system in paying losses. It also examines gaps in insurance coverage that were exposed by Hurricane Sandy and examines the storm's effects on general insurance market conditions and on insurance rates in New York City. We used quantitative data when available. When quantitative data were not available, we relied on the observations of the insurance industry experts interviewed.

Flood Insurance Claims and Payments for Hurricane Sandy

National Flood Insurance Program Claims and Payments

Data on individual NFIP claims for New York City are used to analyze claims and payments due to Hurricane Sandy. The data are current though February 2013. More claims may still be reported to the NFIP, but we did not make any estimates regarding those potential claims. Claims with a loss date between October 27 and November 2, 2012 (inclusive), were attributed to Hurricane Sandy.[1] Claims were matched with the pertinent NFIP policy and linked with the appropriate property parcel using the methods described in Chapter Two.

As of February 2013, the NFIP had received 16,264 claims for losses in New York City attributed to Hurricane Sandy (see Table 3.1). Of those, 81 percent had been closed, some without payment, and 19 percent remained open. After application of the policy deductible, payments on open and closed claims total nearly $750 million through February, with the vast majority (93 percent) for building coverage as opposed to contents coverage.[2] The average payment on closed claims is approximately

---

[1] The peak of the storm hit New York City on October 29, and daily NFIP claims were higher in New York City between October 27 and November 2 than for surrounding dates. To account for damage in the run-up to Hurricane Sandy, as well as in the days immediately following the storm peak (and possible errors in coding the loss date), we attributed claims with loss dates during this period to Hurricane Sandy.

[2] Interim payments can be made on open claims, resulting in the nonzero payments on open claims in Table 3.1.

Table 3.1
National Flood Insurance Program Claims in New York City for Hurricane Sandy, by Claim Status, as of February 28, 2013

Claim Status	Number of Claims	Payments on Building Coverage ($ millions)	Payments on Contents Coverage ($ millions)	Total Payments ($ millions)	Average Total Payment per Claim (dollars)
Closed					
Closed with payment	12,153	611.4	42.6	654.0	53,814
Closed without payment	665	0.0	0.0	0.0	0
Open	3,446	85.6	10.3	95.9	27,829
Total	16,264	697.0	52.9	749.9	46,102

SOURCE: NFIP claim data.

$54,000.[3] These figures include payments on claims both in and outside the high-risk areas of the 2007 FIRM.

Overall, claims were filed on 63 percent of the NFIP policies in New York City (16,264 of the 25,916 policies). Hurricane Sandy reached well beyond the high-risk areas of the 2007 FIRM: Claims were filed on 81 percent of the 13,307 NFIP policies inside the high-risk areas and 43 percent of the 12,609 policies outside the high-risk areas.

Table 3.2 shows the number of NFIP claims, total claim payments (after application of the deductible), and average payment by structure category. Consistent with the distribution of policies by structure type shown in Table 2.7 in Chapter Two, the bulk of claims and claim payments are for one- to four-family dwellings.

Table 3.3 provides detail on the distribution of building damage as reported on closed NFIP claims. Some have proposed that the NFIP offer policyholders the option to select higher deductibles, and the figures in Table 3.3 provide insight into how frequently losses would exceed different deductible levels for a storm similar to Hurricane Sandy. As can be calculated from the table, building damage was $10,000 or less on 10 percent of closed claims and $25,000 or less on 29 percent of closed claims.

Changes in the maximum policy limits on building coverage have also been proposed over the years. Table 3.4 provides some insight into the consequences of increasing the maximum limit. The table reports the number of closed claims that paid to the limit on the particular policy. The limit is chosen by the insured or set as required by

---

[3] FEMA reports through June 30, 2013, that it has paid $7.12 billion on 126,895 claims for all losses related to Hurricane Sandy. These figures cover claims across the region, both in and outside of New York City (FEMA, "Significant Flood Events as of June 30, 2013," c. July 2013b).

Table 3.2
National Flood Insurance Program Claims in New York City for Hurricane Sandy, by Structure Type, as of February 28, 2013

Structure Type	Number of Claims	Total Payments ($ millions)	Average Payment per Claim ($)
Residential			
One- to four-family dwelling	13,307	593.7	44,616
Condominium	245	10.8	44,082
Multifamily dwelling	703	22.9	32,575
Mixed-use property	435	28.8	66,207
Commercial			
Commercial and industrial	437	38.3	87,643
Transportation and utility	118	5.7	48,305
Condominium	34	3.3	97,059
Other	436	24.0	55,046
Missing	549	22.3	40,619
Total	16,264	749.9	46,102

SOURCE: NFIP data merged with New York City parcel data.
NOTE: Because of rounding, total payments do not sum precisely.

the MPR and may not equal the maximum available from the NFIP (see Table 2.9 in Chapter Two for the distribution of policy limits in New York for one- to four-family structures). But even so, few policies on residential structures paid to the policy limit. The policy limit was reached in only 4 percent of claims on one- to four-family dwellings. The percentages were higher for multifamily and mixed-use properties but still were below 20 percent. Increasing the maximum NFIP policy limit would thus not result in higher claim payments for the vast majority of one- to four-family homes for a Hurricane Sandy–type event, given current purchasing behavior.

Private Insurer Claims and Payments
Information on flood-related losses paid by private insurers due to Hurricane Sandy is not readily available. The three major catastrophe modeling firms (AIR, EQECAT, and Risk Management Solutions [RMS]) provided estimates of privately insured loss in the weeks following the event. These estimates ranged from $10 billion to $25 billion, with the average of the midpoints of the three estimated ranges equal to $18.8 billion.[4] The

[4]   Robert P. Hartwig, "The Insurance Industry's Response to Superstorm Sandy: Putting the Northeast on the Road to Recovery," Washington, D.C.: Insurance Information Institute, press briefing, December 10, 2012.

Table 3.3
Number of Closed National Flood Insurance Program
Claims in New York City for Hurricane Sandy, by
Amount of Building Damage, as of February 28, 2013

Building Damage ($)	Number of Claims	Percentage
0 to 5,000	857	7
5,001 to 10,000	428	3
10,001 to 25,000	2,492	19
25,001 to 50,000	4,430	35
50,001 to 100,000	3,640	28
100,001 to 250,000	818	6
250,001 to 500,000	102	1
500,001 to 1 million	37	<0.5
>1 million	14	<0.5
Total	12,818	100

SOURCE: NFIP data.

estimates do not include payments by the NFIP, and they do not separate private insurance payment for flood losses from those for wind losses. As discussed in Chapter Two, private residential policies typically exclude flood coverage, and commercial policies often do. Thus, the private losses are mostly likely predominantly wind related. These numbers also cover all regions affected by the storm, not just New York City.

Gaps in Insurance Coverage

Hurricane Sandy revealed gaps in the coverage available for flood damage, and it is important to recognize those weaknesses in order to improve New York City's resilience to the next event. In this section, we review the gaps in coverage and some other issues identified in our interviews.

Gaps in Residential Coverage

NFIP policies provide only limited basement coverage, do not cover additional living expenses, and do not cover claims due to earth movement under the slab even if that movement was due to water.

For comparison, private insurer losses were $48.7 billion for Hurricane Katrina and $26.5 billion for Hurricane Andrew (adjusted to 2012 dollars).

Table 3.4
National Flood Insurance Program Payments in New York City Following Hurricane Sandy for Damage to Buildings That Are at the Policy Limit for Building Coverage

Total Claim Payment ($)	Number of Closed Claims[a]	Number of Claims at Policy Limit	Percentage of Closed Claims That Paid to Policy Limit
Residential			
One- to four-family dwelling	10,875	383	4
Condominium	116	9	8
Multifamily dwelling	213	35	16
Mixed-use property	157	29	18
Commercial			
Commercial and industrial	144	44	31
Transportation and utility	52	7	13
Condominium	6	4	67
Other	225	24	11
Missing	365	44	12
Total	12,153	579	5

SOURCE: NFIP data.

[a] Excluding claims closed without payment.

Basement Coverage

For residential homeowners in New York City, the lack of full basement coverage in the NFIP leaves many homeowners exposed to substantial loss. In a city where square footage is at a premium but footprints must remain small, basements are common in residential and commercial properties. If a property with a basement experiences flooding, the first place that will be flooded is the basement. A flood insurance policy that limits coverage for a common cause of loss is less valuable to the purchaser—but it is also less expensive. Whether policyholders would find basement coverage attractive at actuarially fair rates is an open question. (More information on the basement coverage provided by the NFIP is given in Appendix A.)

Complaints were widespread among those we interviewed about the definition of *basement* under the NFIP. This was true for both residential and commercial properties. Interviewees thought it inappropriate that a floor that is only one or two steps down from ground level can be considered a basement under the NFIP. Interviewees believed that policyholders would benefit from a clear, simple definition of *basement* in the NFIP.[5]

Lack of Additional Living Expenses

If a property does experience flooding, an NFIP policy will not cover the costs of temporary housing. Like basement coverage, coverage for temporary housing, if it existed, would frequently pay out following a large flood event. But again, whether consumers would be willing to pay for coverage that includes additional living expenses would depend on how much the premium increased.

Lack of Coverage for Earth Movement

The NFIP covers direct physical loss to buildings by flooding but does not cover damage caused by earth movement under the slab of a house even if the earth movement was caused by flooding. This gap in coverage has resulted in several hundred homeowners in New York with denied NFIP claims or only partial payment. New York State has announced that it will fully compensate homeowners for damage caused by earth movement.[6]

Gaps in Commercial Coverage

The biggest coverage gaps for commercial properties in the NFIP relate to the lack of basement coverage, lack of business-interruption or business-expense coverage, and inadequate policy limits for mixed-use buildings. Interviews revealed that commercial property owners would like to see the NFIP move to providing replacement-cost coverage rather than actual-cash-value coverage. Turning to private policies, we see that the biggest gap in the flood coverage provided by private insurers was that business interruption or extra expense did not pay in cases in which the businesses did not suffer physical flood damage on the premises. We also heard of inconsistent applications of the civil-authority-closure coverage, which is discussed in more detail below.

Lack of Basement Coverage in National Flood Insurance Program Policies

Many commercial properties in the city have basements and either use them (e.g., laundry facilities in apartment buildings, storage) or rent them out. The lack of basement coverage for commercial buildings reduces the attractiveness of NFIP policies, although policyholders may not be willing to pay the price for better coverage.

---

[5]   The NFIP defines *basement* as "any area of the building, including any sunken room or sunken portion of a room, having its floor below ground level (subgrade) on all sides" (NFIP, "Resources: Glossary," last updated September 26, 2013b). This definition appears straightforward, although perhaps not what many would like it to be.

[6]   See Office of the Governor, "Governor Cuomo Announces Housing Recovery Program to Compensate Homeowners for Repairs of Damage Due to Storms Irene, Lee and Sandy," press release, September 28, 2013; David B. Caruso, "New York to Compensate Storm Victims for NFIP's 'Earth Movement' Exclusion," *Insurance Journal*, September 30, 2013; and Laura Schofer, "Cuomo: State Will Compensate for 'Earth Movement' Loss," *Baldwin Herald*, October 2, 2013.

Lack of Business-Interruption Coverage in National Flood Insurance Program Policies

Small to medium-sized businesses likely hold the bulk of the NFIP commercial policies. These businesses do not have the financial resources of larger firms and have a difficult time surviving closures of more than a week. The lack of business-interruption and business-expense coverage within the NFIP was a burden for firms of this size. Some private insurers provide flood policies that cover business interruption if the damage occurs on the premises, but these policies are expensive for smaller firms.

Gaps in National Flood Insurance Program Coverage for Mixed-Use Buildings

Under the NFIP, if the building occupancy is more than 25 percent commercial, the building is considered commercial and has access to the commercial policy limits ($500,000 for building coverage and $500,000 for contents coverage). The opposite is also true: If the building is more than 75 percent residential in use, it is considered a residential building, and the commercial portions are held to residential policy limits ($250,000 building and $100,000 contents). New York City has numerous apartment and condominium buildings that have business firms on the first floor and more than three residential floors above so would be considered residential. NFIP coverage limits are frequently not large compared to the value of the property at risk in the commercial portions of these types of buildings. Private insurers offer flood policies that better fit the needs of these types of buildings but are more expensive.

Lack of National Flood Insurance Program Coverage for Replacement Costs

Another shortcoming in the NFIP policy for commercial property identified in our interviews is the lack of coverage for replacement costs. Brokers and agents said that commercial property owners desire to have replacement-cost valuation rather than actual cash value. This aspect of NFIP coverage is another deterrent to the take-up of flood insurance by commercial firms.

Lack of Business-Interruption and Extra-Expense Coverage in the Absence of a Direct Loss

Even for those commercial properties that had private flood insurance that included business-interruption coverage, for many, the business-interruption coverage was never triggered because the loss did not occur on their own premises. This came as a surprise to many property owners. Hurricane Sandy disrupted many businesses that did not experience a direct loss. For example, if a neighboring building experienced severe flooding and the utility company cut off power to the policyholder's portion of the block, preventing that policyholder from being able to conduct business, the business-interruption or extra-expense insurance might not trigger because the damage did not occur on the policyholder's premises. Such coverage is available through what are referred to as *contingent business-interruption policies*. However, these policies are not always available for a particular property and can be very expensive.

Variations in Application of Civil-Authority-Closure Coverage

According to those we interviewed, experiences differed regarding whether insurers paid for business-interruption losses or the additional business expenses due to Hurricane Sandy when a building was closed or made inaccessible due to actions by the police or other civil authority. In some cases, insurers paid the claims; in others, they did not. Some insurers covered business-interruption claims for properties in areas that were closed by the city or by the police due to flooding. Other insurers did not pay those claims, citing that the trigger for the closure was flood, which is not a covered peril in their policies. Even if a property owner had flood insurance in addition to business-interruption and extra-expense coverage, insurance did not necessarily pay if the water did not reach the building. In other cases, insurers made payments. Differences were driven by details in the policy language, the particularities of each situation, and judgment calls by different insurers to pay or not to pay.

Other Issues
Shortage of Adjusters

There did not appear to be enough adjusters to handle the volume of claims related to Hurricane Sandy. National carriers seemed to have fared better because they had access to a nationwide network of claim adjusters. The smaller, more-regional carriers had a difficult time finding enough adjusters to assess damage in a timely manner. Independent adjusters tended to work for the national insurers rather than the smaller insurers because of the prospect of future work. This situation created particular problems for the smaller insurers. Although the Department of Financial Services required insurers to adjust claims within six days instead of the typical 15 days after Hurricane Sandy, the size and scale of the storm and a lack of qualified adjusters made this physically impossible for some insurers.

NFIP claims must be adjusted by a certified flood damage adjuster, but these adjusters are more common in areas that experience frequent hurricanes and other flood-related events. As a consequence, the adjusters for Hurricane Sandy tended to come from the South. Although experienced in adjusting hurricane losses, these adjusters were not accustomed to the high cost of materials and labor in New York City. Some agents reported that the adjusters did not seem to acknowledge the higher costs under normal circumstances in New York City, let alone in an environment of constrained supply and increased demand.

Lack of Accounting for Disaster Capitalism

As referenced above, the price of both materials and labor can increase in the wake of a disaster as a result of constrained supply and high demand (often referred to as *demand surge*). Some agents we interviewed observed that private insurers did not fully consider the higher prices that immediate demands can create. For example, suppose a laborer from North Carolina offers to remove the tree from the top of a house right now for $1,200. If the homeowner has not been able to reach any tree-removal services and fears further damage due to rain, he or she pays the $1,200. The homeowner submits the claim to his or her insurer, which tells the homeowner that it will reimburse only $800, which is the standard cost for tree removal.

Lack of Knowledge About the Availability of National Flood Insurance Program Commercial Flood Insurance

Some of those we interviewed believed that the low take-up rate of NFIP commercial flood policies among the small and medium-sized firms most suited for NFIP coverage was due to the fact that many of these firms did not realize that such coverage was available. It was suggested that a better marketing campaign geared to smaller businesses might help improve take-up.

Hurricane Sandy's Impact on the Price and Availability of Flood Insurance

A storm of Hurricane Sandy's magnitude might have impacts on the insurance industry as a whole by depleting industry reserves. Faced with large claim payments that deplete insurer capital, insurers may be less willing to write coverage in a wide range of insurance lines, thus reducing availability and driving up prices. Insurers may also reassess the risk of hurricane-related losses, both in the areas affected by the storm and in the hurricane-exposed area more broadly. In this section, we investigate Hurricane Sandy's impact on the overall insurance market, as well as on price and availability of insurance in New York City. Our analysis focuses on privately provided wind and flood insurance. Changes in NFIP rates, which proceed on administrative schedules not linked to Hurricane Sandy, are discussed in Chapter Four.

Impact on Overall Insurance Industry

Many of the observations by the insurers and insurance brokers about Hurricane Sandy's impact on insurance pricing are consistent with the conclusion reached by Advisen in its January 2013 white paper.[7] Advisen concluded that Hurricane Sandy will, at worst, affect insurer earnings but will have no meaningful overall impact on industry capital (surplus). Advisen projects that, unless losses from Hurricane Sandy are much larger than currently estimated or additional disasters occur, the U.S. property and casualty industry will finish 2013 with modest profit, and policyholders' surplus will hold steady. It believes that Hurricane Sandy will be a catalyst for short-term rate hikes, especially for property in catastrophe-exposed regions. Nonetheless, Hurricane Sandy–related losses probably will not be sufficient to propel sharply higher premiums across the industry as a whole for a sustained period of time. Advisen concluded

---

[7] Advisen is a privately owned, independent provider of news, data, and risk analytics to the commercial insurance industry.

that, although premiums may trend upward in the short term—especially for business property in catastrophe-prone regions—the property and casualty insurance market remains abundantly capitalized, which should cushion the financial impact and avoid the type of hard market conditions seen in 2001 and 2002.[8]

Consistently with this view, one of the insurers interviewed expected Hurricane Sandy's long-term impact to be modest. According to this observer, insurers already heavily exposed in the New York City area will withdraw some capacity, but that capacity will quickly be replaced by other insurers and other sources of capital. With the advent of hedge-fund and pension-fund backing, the catastrophe insurance market is viewed as very resilient. Another insurer we interviewed observed that, after a bad 2011, many catastrophe insurers were planning to increase rates in 2012. But the relatively small number of catastrophic events in 2012 prior to Hurricane Sandy led them to forgo planned rate increases. Hurricane Sandy led many to revise that thinking; according to this observer, they may again seek to raise rates. However, it appears that reinsurers were generally disappointed by the level of rate increase they were able to achieve for the January 1, 2013, renewals. According to this observer, insurers were concerned that prices would decline in 2013.

Other interviewees saw the trends a bit differently. A few national brokers noted that they believed that the overall property insurance price has increased from 10 to 20 percent as a result of Hurricane Sandy—and not just in the areas damaged by the storm.

The Council of Insurance Agents and Brokers (CIAB) conducts a quarterly survey of its members regarding how premium rates on commercial policies have changed. Members are asked to characterize the premium changes for similar coverage that is renewed with the same carrier or moved to a new carrier during the quarter. Results from two quarters prior to Hurricane Sandy through two quarters post–Hurricane Sandy are presented in Table 3.5. There is little indication that Hurricane Sandy had a significant impact on the prices of commercial property, business interruption, or general liability insurance nationally. The figures do suggest that prices of privately provided commercial flood insurance have accelerated post–Hurricane Sandy, particularly in the Northeast. Of course, care must be taken to separate effects of Hurricane Sandy from those not related to the hurricane that may have simultaneously occurred.

Impact on Private Flood Insurance Prices and Availability in New York City

After Hurricane Sandy, a moratorium was put into place by the New York State Department of Financial Services on policy cancellations and on significant rate increases in

---

[8]   Advisen, "The State of the Commercial Property/Casualty Insurance Market," January 2013, p. 2. In a hard market, insurance prices increase, and coverage can become more difficult to obtain.

Table 3.5
Changes in Commercial Insurance Premiums by Line of Insurance (percentage of Council of Insurance Agents and Brokers survey respondents reporting rate increases greater than 10 percent)

	2012			2013	
Insurance Line	Q2	Q3	Q4	Q1	Q2
Commercial property					
U.S.	28	17	21	21	17
Northeast	21	7	13	16	18
Business interruption					
U.S.	5	4	5	3	3
Northeast	14	0	6	0	0
Flood insurance					
U.S.	10	7	12	21	21
Northeast	14	0	25	42	18
General liability					
U.S.	4	7	1	5	4
Northeast	0	0	0	5	6

SOURCES: CIAB, "Commercial P/C Pricing Took Leap in Second Quarter, According to Council Survey," news release, July 31, 2012a; CIAB, "Commercial P/C Pricing Slowed in Third Quarter, According to the Council's Survey," news release, November 1, 2012b; CIAB, "Commercial P/C Pricing Rose 4th Quarter; Underwriting Remained Tight, According to the Council's Survey," news release, February 5, 2013a; CIAB, "Commercial P/C Pricing Continued Upward Trend in First Quarter, According to the Council's Survey," news release, April 18, 2013b; CIAB, "Commercial P/C Pricing Increases Slowed in Second Quarter, According to CIAB Survey," news release, July 23, 2013c.

the admitted market.[9] The moratorium was gradually lifted by location, with the final area removed from the moratorium in early April 2013. Insurers wanting to change terms, conditions, or pricing more than 10 percent had to give 60-day notice plus mailing time, but notices could not be sent until the moratorium ended. As a result, at the

---

[9]   Admitted carriers submit their applications, policy forms, endorsements, and rating structure for approval by the New York State Department of Financial Services. If the coverage they seek is not available from admitted insurers, individuals and businesses can turn to the nonadmitted (or surplus-lines) insurers for coverage.

time of our interviews in February and March 2013, admitted insurers had not had the opportunity yet to make much in the way of rate or coverage changes as a result of Hurricane Sandy. According to those with whom we spoke, insurers saw little new business after the storm (because existing policies could not be canceled) and, during the moratorium period, renewals typically came in at a 7- to 10-percent increase.

Our interviews indicated that private insurers are revisiting their entire books of business related to flooding post–Hurricane Sandy and are moving toward limiting their exposure. Some are doing this primarily by reducing coverage limits rather than dropping properties. The premiums will be the same for less coverage. Some insurers will now provide flood coverage only in excess of other coverage (they will take only the layers greater than $25 million on large commercial properties, for example). Others noted that they are seeing many domestic carriers that previously provided flood coverage to businesses now excluding that coverage from their package policies. Others will still offer flood coverage but not in high-risk areas. This is resulting in brokers having to reach out to international markets where they can still find flood coverage. Although coverage is becoming more expensive, it appears to be available in the United States from non-U.S. insurers.

One commercial broker estimated that the average price in New York City post–Hurricane Sandy had risen about 20 percent for properties in high-risk areas. For low-risk properties with good elevation, the increase might be 10 to 15 percent. For high-risk properties that experienced a loss, that increase might be closer to 35 or 40 percent.

Some interviewees explained that the RMS 11 hurricane model, which was adopted in the summer of 2011, did a fairly good job of predicting an event like Hurricane Sandy.[10] As a result, premiums may not increase in some areas post–Hurricane Sandy. However, according to an insurer we interviewed, Hurricane Sandy revealed vulnerabilities in New York City that were not anticipated by the RMS model, so adjustments in price are still happening within the city.

Despite rising prices, signs indicate that the New York City insurance marketplace remains competitive. Some established carriers are attempting to capture new business and are offering attractive prices to secure that business. Some relatively new carriers are offering very attractive rates to increase market share. Some of these new carriers experienced few losses due to Hurricane Sandy, and this lack of substantial losses is likely to keep them aggressive and the marketplace competitive for the near future.

---

[10] RMS's North Atlantic Hurricane Model predicts hurricane landfall rates and the associated damage. Version 11 was released in 2011, and Version 13 was released in the summer of 2013.

CHAPTER FOUR

Impact of National Flood Insurance Program Reform and Flood-Map Changes on New York City

In this chapter, we consider the effects of recent NFIP legislative reforms and flood-map updates for the residents and businesses of New York City. Both of these changes are independent of Hurricane Sandy and will have major effects on the premiums charged on NFIP policies. We begin by describing provisions in BW-12 to reduce insurance-rate subsidies in the NFIP and the likely effect of these changes on the price of flood insurance. We then describe the revisions to the FIRM for New York City. We discuss changes in the number of properties in high-risk flood zones and the number of those properties that will be required to purchase flood insurance. We conclude by examining the effects of flood-map changes on the NFIP premiums paid by property owners.

The Effects of the Biggert-Waters Flood Insurance Reform Act on National Flood Insurance Program Premiums for Pre-FIRM Structures

Besides reauthorizing the NFIP for five years, BW-12 is designed to make the NFIP financially stronger. To do so, BW-12 phases out subsidies on certain classes of pre-FIRM structures. In the case of New York City, these are structures that were built prior to the release of the first FIRM for the city in November 1983.

Elimination of Subsidized Rates on Some Pre-FIRM Structures

The following is a summary of the changes related to the subsidized pre-FIRM rates as described in Section 100205 of BW-12 (descriptions of zone designations can be found in Table A.5 in Appendix A):

- Effective January 1, 2013, for both new and renewing policyholders, pre-FIRM, nonprimary[1] residences in high-risk flood areas will see 25-percent rate increases annually until rates reflect the NFIP's estimate of full risk.
- Beginning October 1, 2013, pre-FIRM residences in a high-risk area or Zone D that have experienced severe loss or repetitive losses will see 25-percent rate increases annually until rates reflect true risk.[2]
- Also beginning October 1, 2013, pre-FIRM nonresidential buildings in high-risk flood areas or Zone D will see 25-percent rate increases annually until rates reflect true risk.
- Also beginning October 1, 2013, pre-FIRM buildings in high-risk flood areas or Zone D that were not previously insured, were newly purchased, or had a lapsed policy on or after July 6, 2012 (October 4, 2012 for lapsed policies) will pay full-risk rate.[3]

FEMA estimates that approximately 250,000 of the approximately 4.5 million NFIP policies nationwide (6 percent) will be affected by changes summarized in the first three changes. Another 580,000 (13 percent) will be affected when an insured property is sold or the policy lapses (the last change).[4]

As shown in Table 2.4 in Chapter Two, a high percentage of structures in New York City's high-risk areas are pre-FIRM. For one- to four-family structures, the percentage is 78. Thus, 78 percent of one- to four-family structures will potentially be affected by the elimination of subsidies on pre-FIRM structures.[5]

---

[1]   FEMA defines *primary structure* as one in which the policyholder lives for at least 80 percent of the policy year. Also note that replacement-cost coverage is available only for primary residences (and even those must be insured to at least 80 percent of replacement cost).

[2]   No areas in New York City are mapped as Zone D. A repetitive-loss residence is a residence that has received two or more claim payments of more than $1,000 from the NFIP within any rolling ten-year period (FEMA, "Repetitive Loss," August 15, 2007).

   A severe-repetitive residence is a residence (1) that has at least four NFIP claim payments (including building and contents) greater than $5,000 each, with the cumulative amount of such claim payments exceeding $20,000, or (2) for which at least two separate claim payments (building payments only) have been made with the cumulative amount of the building portion of such claims exceeding the market value of the building. For either condition, at least two of the referenced claims must have occurred within any ten-year period and must be greater than ten days apart (FEMA, "Severe Repetitive Loss Program," last updated August 2, 2013c).

[3]   So, if the property owner obtained a policy on or after July 6, 2012, it will have to be actuarially rated at renewal after October 1, 2013. An elevation certificate (EC) will be required to determine the rate. FEMA has what is known as provisional rates that do not require an EC, but those rates can be used for only one year.

[4]   About 20 percent of the approximately 4.5 million NFIP contracts nationwide are on pre-FIRM structures (FEMA, *National Flood Insurance Program: Specific Rating Guidelines*, October 2013e).

[5]   Note that not all pre-FIRM structures receive subsidized NFIP rates. Pre-FIRM structures outside the high-risk areas are not subsidized. Even some in the high-risk areas are not subsidized. Pre-FIRM structures that have demonstrated compliance with the current FIRM or any earlier FIRM can be rated using a zone and elevation rate and do not receive the pre-FIRM subsidized rate. Some may have been outside the special flood hazard area

How many of the pre-FIRM structures in New York City will be affected by changes required by BW-12? Data from FEMA show that there are 4,044 properties in New York City that are considered severe-loss or repetitive-loss properties. Estimates of the turnover of structures in New York City's high-risk areas have not been developed, although the U.S. Government Accountability Office (GAO) analysis of BW-12 assumes that between 11 and 14 percent of pre-FIRM homes will be sold per year nationwide.[6] We have not been able to determine the number of nonprimary pre-FIRM residences in New York City's high-risk flood zones.

More than 85 percent of the approximately 4,300 business structures in New York City's high-risk area are pre-FIRM (see Tables 2.1 and 2.4 in Chapter Two), and those with pre-FIRM rates will see their rates increase 25 percent annually beginning in October 2013 until full-risk rates are reached. Those that do not already have NFIP policies will immediately need to pay the full-risk rates should they purchase NFIP insurance.

Table 4.1 provides some examples of what the rates for pre-FIRM single-family homes will be after the BW-12 rate changes are fully phased in.[7] How much rates will change for homes no longer eligible for pre-FIRM rates will depend on a variety of factors, including flood zone and the elevation of the home relative to the BFE. As shown in the first row of Table 4.1, the subsidized pre-FIRM rate for $200,000 in building coverage and $80,000 in contents coverage is $2,922 for a home without a basement in a high-risk flood zone (Zone AE). If the lowest floor of the home is 1 foot below BFE, the unsubsidized rate is $5,090 (which is the same rate as for post-FIRM structures with −1 elevation in Zone AE). Note that, if the lowest floor of a home in Zone AE is at BFE, the full-risk rate ($1,722) is lower than the subsidized rate. Many pre-FIRM homes in such a situation have presumably already switched to the full-risk rate.

The number of pre-FIRM homes in high-risk areas in New York City that are below BFE is not known. Structure elevation is not required to price a policy on a pre-FIRM structure, and FEMA does not collect this information.

The Impact of Flood-Map Changes on New York City

Updating the FIRM used by the NFIP could have a major effect on the flood insurance premiums paid by New York City's residents and businesses. In this section, we

---

(SFHA) according to an earlier FIRM and are now using a grandfathered X zone rate or the Preferred Risk Policy (PRP) extension rate (discussed later in this chapter).

[6] GAO, *Flood Insurance: More Information Needed on Subsidized Properties*, Washington, D.C., GAO-13-607, July 2013, pp. 14–15.

[7] Premiums were calculated using Torrent Technologies' online flood insurance rating system. Torrent Technologies specializes in providing business services to write-your-own companies within the NFIP.

Table 4.1
Examples of Annual National Flood Insurance Program Premium Changes for Homes That Lose Subsidies

Zone	Elevation	Subsidized Premium Paid Prior to BW-12[a]	Full-Risk Premium Paid After BW-12 Phased In[b]	Difference
AE	−1	2,922	5,090	2,168
AE	0	2,922	1,722	−1,200
VE	−1	6,016	9,530	3,514
VE	0	6,016	7,094	1,078

SOURCE: Torrent Technologies' online flood insurance rating system.

NOTE: Pre-FIRM subsidy amount is based on rates set to take effect on October 1, 2013. The estimates are for a pre-FIRM single-family home with no basement or enclosure and $200,000 in building coverage and $80,000 in contents coverage.

[a] $2,000 building deductible and $2,000 contents deductible.

[b] $1,000 building deductible and $1,000 contents deductible.

first describe the FIRM update process and then estimate the number of structures added to the high-risk areas by the PWM for the new FIRM. We provide estimates of the take-up rates for structures added to the high-risk areas and conclude by developing examples of how NFIP premiums in New York City might change under the new map.

The Flood Insurance Rate Map Update Process

In 2010, well before Hurricane Sandy, FEMA began the transition from its Flood Map Modernization Initiative to its Risk Mapping, Assessment, and Planning (Risk MAP) initiative, which has a vision of delivering "quality data that increases public awareness and leads to action that reduces risk to life and property."[8] Through Risk MAP, FEMA has shifted from countywide mapping to a watershed approach and is now remapping all four U.S. coasts (Pacific, Gulf, Atlantic, and Great Lakes).

FEMA Region 2 is currently overseeing the remapping of the New Jersey coastline, as well as New York City and Westchester County. Its mapping contractor, Risk Assessment, Mapping, and Planning Partners (RAMPP), began its analysis for New York City in September 2010 and has a target date of the fall of 2013 for the release of the preliminary FIRM for New York City. Besides FEMA holding the required consultation coordination officer (CCO) meeting with public officials when the preliminary FIRM is released, there will typically also be public open houses for local residents and business owners to see the map and talk with officials. The next step is a 90-day appeals period in which anyone (e.g., homeowner, developer, the NFIP community)

---

[8]   FEMA, "What Is Risk MAP?" October 2012.

can submit an appeal that is scientifically based to show that the map is incorrect.[9] Once all appeals have been answered and resolved,[10] the final map will be processed, and a letter of final determination (LFD) will be issued. This gives the NFIP community six months to pass an ordinance that adopts the new FIRM. After that six-month period ends, this FIRM becomes the new effective flood map, and any changes in flood insurance requirements due to changes in flood zone or BFE take effect. The date the new FIRM will become effective in New York City is unknown; it depends on the number of appeals submitted that need to be resolved. A target date may be early 2015.

The coastal floodplain study was performed using the latest storm-surge modeling (ADvanced CIRCulation [ADCIRC] and Simulating WAves Nearshore [SWAN][11]) along with updated bathymetry and coastal elevation data, including lidar[12] data from New York City. There are many steps that go into mapping the coastal hazard areas, including terrain processing, the storm-surge analysis, field reconnaissance, primary frontal dune delineation, analyzing for storm-induced erosion, and overland wave height and run-up analysis. The storm-surge analysis identifies what is known as still-water elevations (SWELs) and defines the coastal hazard areas. To establish the BFEs, a program called Wave Height Analysis for Flood Insurance Studies (WHAFIS) is run that takes into account wave setup (the increase in water level) and starting wave heights. Modeling is also done of wave run-up (the vertical height of waves above the stillwater elevation crashing against a beach or structure). When Hurricane Sandy hit, FEMA wanted property owners along the coast to have updated information to inform rebuilding because initial results indicated that high-risk flood hazard areas and BFEs would be increasing in many areas.

Unfortunately, the preliminary FIRM was not yet ready to be released because the overland wave analysis had not been completed. Instead, an ABFE map for New York City was issued in two phases. Phase I was released on January 28, 2013, and included all the open shoreline sections of New York City (South Queens, Southern Brooklyn, the southeast shore of Staten Island, and the portion of the Bronx adjacent to Long Island Sound). Phase II was released on February 25, 2013, for all the sheltered shoreline areas of New York City. This included the west and north shores of Staten Island, the rest of Brooklyn on New York Harbor and along the East River, the portions of the Bronx and Queens on the upper East River, and all of Manhattan.

---

[9]   "Communities" can join the NFIP. A community has planning and building-code authority within its jurisdiction. New York City is an NFIP community. NFIP policies are available to businesses and residents in communities that have joined the NFIP.

[10]   If there is a change in BFE, flood zones, or floodway, additional outreach meetings and notices will need to be taken and issued.

[11]   ADCIRC is a model of oceanic, coastal, and estuarine waters.

[12]   Lidar is a remote sensing method to determine ground elevation from an airplane.

Consequently, the message was for property owners to rebuild based on this updated flood risk information and not the current 2007 FIRM, which was based on coastal data and modeling from the early 1980s. Using the ABFEs would not only help reduce future flood risk but also help avoid paying higher flood insurance premiums when the new map became effective, especially because, as discussed in the section on rate grandfathering later in this chapter, the grandfathering option would eventually be eliminated when FEMA implemented Section 100207 of BW-12 (discussed below).

In June 2013, FEMA released the PWM for the new FIRM. The PWM is based on the same underlying storm modeling as the ABFE but with the WHAFIS and wave modeling incorporated into the analysis. The PWM is now considered the best available data and is the standard to which property owners are recommended to rebuild. The analysis in this chapter uses the PWM. This map still does not identify regions subject to riverine, as opposed to coastal, flooding. However, the missing areas are likely relatively moderate in size. In the 2007 FIRM, only 2.7 square miles of the 33 square miles in the high-risk flood areas (8 percent) were subject to riverine flooding. The following analysis of the PWM does not include areas subject to riverine flooding, but excluding the riverine areas will not have a great deal of impact on the findings. The high-risk areas subject to coastal flooding in the PWM are shown in Figure 4.1, along with the parts of those areas that are already in the 2007 FIRM. As mentioned earlier, the preliminary FIRM that will include the riverine areas is expected in the fall of 2013 and will be available for public comment and appeals.

Extent of the High-Risk Flood Zones in the Preliminary Work Map

The PWM significantly expands the high-risk flood zones in New York City. Table 4.2 reveals that the PWM roughly doubles the number of parcels and structures in areas classified as high risk. The percentage of New York City structures that are in high-risk areas rises to 6.8 percent, from 3.6 percent in the 2007 FIRM (see last row of Table 4.2 and, in Chapter Two, Table 2.3).

The structures added to the high-risk zones were not required to comply with building codes for structures in a floodplain. This holds true both for pre-FIRM and post-FIRM structures. Table 2.4 in Chapter Two shows that there are 28,600 pre-FIRM structures in the high-risk areas of the 2007 FIRM, none of which was built to floodplain standards. The structures added to the high-risk areas were also not built to floodplain standards. Taking into account the fact that some high-risk areas in the 2007 FIRM are not in the high-risk areas of the PWM, 90 percent of the 67,400 structures in the PWM were not built to floodplain standards. Whether the remaining 10 percent meet floodplain standards depends on how well the floodplain building codes have been enforced since the first FIRM was released in 1983.

Figure 4.1
Areas at High Risk of Coastal Flooding

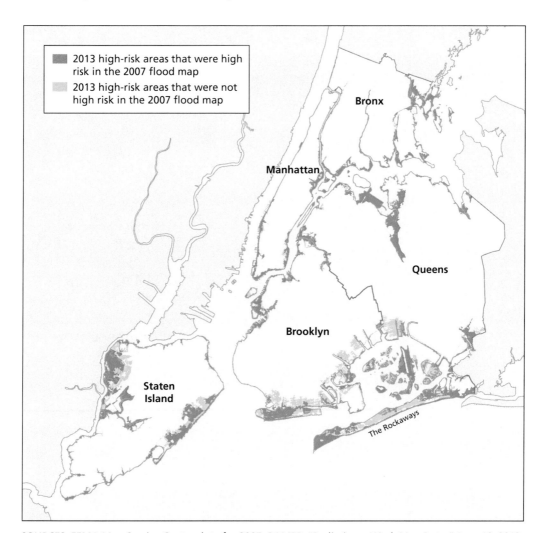

SOURCES: FEMA Map Service Center data for 2007; RAMPP, "Preliminary Work Map Data," June 18, 2013.
NOTE: Areas subject to riverine flooding are not included.
RAND RR328-4.1

Take-Up in High-Risk Areas of the Preliminary Work Map

The expansion of the high-risk area will increase the number of structures subject to the MPR. It will also increase the number of structures in high-risk areas not subject to the MPR, creating greater challenges for efforts to increase take-up rates in areas exposed to flood risk.

To project the number of structures affected by the expansion of the high-risk areas, we first estimate take-up and the percentage of properties known to have mortgages that also have flood insurance policies in the high-risk areas *added* by the PWM.

Table 4.2
Number of Parcels, Structures, and Housing Units in High-Risk Areas of the Preliminary Work Map and 2007 Flood Insurance Risk Map

Structure Type	Parcels			Structures			Housing Units		
	2007 FIRM	PWM	Percentage of All City Parcels in High-Risk Areas of PWM	2007 FIRM	PWM	Percentage of All City Structures in High-Risk Areas of PWM	2007 FIRM	PWM	Percentage of All City Housing Units in High-Risk Areas of PWM
Residential	21,000	47,100	6.3	29,200	58,900	6.5	161,600	244,900	7.2
One- to four-family dwelling	19,100	43,700	6.7	25,800	53,000	6.8	31,400	71,800	6.5
Condominium	100	200	7.8	700	900	7.2	2,500	4,400	6.9
Multifamily dwelling	800	1,500	3.1	1,400	2,700	4.2	86,000	117,900	7.4
Mixed-use dwelling	1,000	1,700	3.5	1,300	2,300	4.1	41,600	50,700	8.1
Commercial	3,500	5,000	9.2	4,300	5,900	10.1	500	600	6.2
Commercial and industrial	2,000	2,900	8.0	2,700	3,800	9.1	400	600	6.2
Transportation and utility	1,500	2,100	11.7	1,600	2,000	12.8	0	0	5.1
Condominium	20	20	8.5	30	30	9.3	0	0	
Other	6,700	7,600	16.4	1,800	2,200	11.3	500	1,000	4.2
Missing	700	900	19.5	400	400	23.8	200	200	88.4
Total	31,900	60,700	7.1	35,700	67,400	6.8	162,700	246,700	7.2

NOTE: Because of rounding, rows might not sum precisely. Numbers have been rounded to the nearest hundred (numbers smaller than 100, to the nearest ten).

The estimates use the same methods as in Chapter Two. We then estimate the number of one- to four-family structures in the PWM that currently do not have flood insurance, by mortgage status.

As expected, the take-up rates in the high-risk areas added to the PWM are very low. As shown in Table 4.3, the take-up rate is 10 percent for one- to four-family homes, with similar take-up rates for the other residential structure types. Also as expected, take-up rates are very low regardless of whether there is a mortgage on the property (see Table 4.4). This is not surprising because households outside the high-risk areas of the 2007 FIRM have not been told they are at risk of flooding and face no MPR until the new map is adopted.

We use estimates of take-up rates, the percentage of parcels with mortgages, and the number of parcels to project the number of structures that lacked flood insurance as of October 2012 in the high-risk areas of the PWM. We distinguish between those that will be required to have flood insurance but currently do not and those that will

Table 4.3
Take-Up of National Flood Insurance Program Policies for One- to Four-Family Structures in the High-Risk Zones Added by the Preliminary Work Map (as of October 31, 2012)

Measure	Estimate
Take-up rate (percentage of structures with NFIP policy) (based on 23,100 parcels)[a]	10
Lower bound for take-up rate (based on 25,877 parcels)	10
Upper bound for take-up rate (based on 25,877 parcels)	11

SOURCE: Merge of NFIP policy file with New York City parcel data.

[a] Based on parcels with one structure.

Table 4.4
Take-Up of National Flood Insurance Program Policies for One- to Four-Family Structures in the High-Risk Zones Added by the Preliminary Work Map, by Mortgage Status (as of October 31, 2012)

Measure	Percentage Estimate[a]
Structures with mortgages (based on 18,436 parcels)	79
Take-up rate for structures with mortgages (based on 14,646 parcels)	10
Take-up rate for structures without mortgages (based on 3,790 parcels)	10

[a] Based on parcels with one structure.

not be required to carry flood insurance. For comparison, results for the 2007 FIRM are also reported. The analysis is done for the entire area covered by the PWM, not just those areas newly classified as high risk.

Table 4.5 presents the assumptions used in the projections and the results. For the 2007 FIRM projection, the assumptions are taken from Tables 2.1, 2.5, and 2.6 in Chapter Two, and the assumptions for the PWM projection are taken from Tables B.1

Table 4.5
Projections of the Number of One- to Four-Family Structures Without Flood Insurance as of October 2012 in the High-Risk Zones of New York City

Measure	2007 FIRM	PWM[a]
Assumption		
Number of structures in high-risk area	25,800	53,000
Take-up rate in high-risk area (percentage)	55	28
Percentage of structures with mortgages	72	65
Percentage of structures with mortgages that have flood insurance	68	35
Percentage of structures without mortgages that have flood insurance	21	16
Projections		
Structures that are or will be required to have flood insurance	18,500	34,500
Have flood insurance	12,600	12,100[b]
Do not have flood insurance	5,900	22,400
Take-up rate (percentage)	68	35
Structures that are not or will not be required to have flood insurance	7,200	18,600
Have flood insurance	1,500	3,000
Do not have flood insurance	5,700	15,600
Take-up rate (percentage)	21	16
Total structures	25,800	53,000
Have flood insurance	14,100	15,000
Do not have flood insurance	11,600	38,000
Take-up rate (percentage)	55	28

NOTE: Structure counts are rounded to the nearest hundred.

[a] Excludes areas subject to riverine flooding.

[b] Less than for the 2007 FIRM because the PWM excludes the riverine areas subject to flooding and the percentage of structures with mortgages was adjusted downward so that weighted take-up rates for structures with and without mortgages equals the overall 28-percent take-up rate. In addition, some high-risk areas in the 2007 FIRM are not high risk in the PWM.

and B.2 in Appendix B (Appendix B includes estimates for the entire PWM, not just those areas added to the PWM). The percentage of structures with mortgages is set so that the take-up rate for all structures in the category matches the weighted take-up rates for those with and without mortgages.[13]

The projections show that a large number of one- to four-family structures in the high-risk areas of the PWM currently do not have flood insurance. As shown in the last group of rows in Table 4.6, 38,000 of the one- to four-family structures in the high-risk areas of the PWM did not have flood insurance as of October 31, 2012. Of the 38,000 that did not have flood insurance, 22,400 structures will be subject to the MPR, and another 15,600 will not be subject to the MPR. Inducing the owners of these 15,600 structures to purchase NFIP coverage will be a challenge for city officials.

Impact of Flood Insurance Rate Map Changes on National Flood Insurance Program Rates

The NFIP premiums of post-FIRM structures depend on the difference between the structure elevation and the BFE. And, as BW-12 pushes pre-FIRM structures to risk-based rates, the BFE will become increasingly relevant for pre-FIRM structures as well. We begin this section by examining the BFEs in the new PWM and then turn to the implications for NFIP rates in New York City.

Changes in Base Flood Elevation

The BFEs in the PWM are significantly higher than those in the 2007 FIRM across much of the high-risk area of the 2007 FIRM. Table 4.6 reports the distribution of the difference between the PWM BFE and the 2007 BFE for those parcels that were in the high-risk areas of the 2007 FIRM.[14] The increases in BFE are substantial. As shown in the first row of the table, the BFE increases 2.3 feet, on average, in the 29,060 parcels that were in the high-risk areas of both the 2007 FIRM and the PWM and for which data are available. The increases range between 2.1 and 3.1 feet for the middle 50 percent of the parcels (the range between the 25th and 75th percentiles), with another 25 percent showing increases greater than 3.1 feet. The changes in Brooklyn, Manhattan, and Queens are similar, with larger increases on Staten Island. The BFE in the Bronx changed little on average, with approximately as many parcels showing an increase in BFE as those showing declines. The increases for parcels with pre-FIRM structures are very similar to the increase for parcels with post-FIRM structures. The

---

[13] This adjustment is required because the take-up rates for parcels with and without mortgages are calculated based on a subset of parcels that differs from that used to calculate the take-up for all parcels regardless of mortgage status.

[14] Data on the BFE for each parcel first in the 2007 FIRM and then in the PWM were provided to RAND by the New York City Department of City Planning. To develop the BFEs for each parcel, the Department of Planning linked floodplain data to tax-lot (parcel) data. For those parcels located within multiple flood zones, the parcel was assigned to the most restrictive zone that made up at least 10 percent of the parcel. BFEs were assigned to each parcel using the same methodology.

Table 4.6
Change in Base Flood Elevation Between the 2007 Flood Insurance Rate Map and Preliminary Work Map (feet)

Parcel Characteristic	Number of Parcels	Mean	Percentile				
			5th	25th	50th	75th	95th
All New York City	29,060	2.3	0.1	2.1	2.1	3.1	4.1
Borough							
Brooklyn	6,645	2.5	1.1	2.1	2.1	3.1	4.1
Bronx	2,650	−0.1	−1.9	−0.9	0.1	0.1	2.1
Manhattan	1,587	1.5	0.1	0.1	2.0	2.1	4.1
Queens	10,559	2.4	0.1	2.1	2.1	3.1	4.1
Staten Island	7,619	3.1	2.1	2.1	3.1	3.1	5.1
Date built							
Pre-FIRM	23,318	2.3	0.1	2.1	2.1	3.1	4.1
Post-FIRM	5,742	2.3	0.1	2.1	2.1	3.1	3.1

NOTE: Calculated for parcels in the high-risk area of both the 2007 FIRM and the PWM.

similar increases indicate that pre-FIRM structures are not located in areas that face BFE increases that are substantially different from those that post-FIRM structures do.

Grandfathering of National Flood Insurance Program Rates

Before examining how the flood-map updates might affect NFIP premiums, it is important to discuss the grandfathering of rates in the NFIP and how the eventual implementation of Section 100207 of BW-12 (elimination of grandfathering) will affect current practices.

Prior to BW-12, residents and businesses were shielded from the adverse consequences of a revised flood map. BW-12 eliminates this so-called grandfathering, and the target date for implementation of the relevant provisions is October 2014, at the earliest. However, as discussed later in this section, many implementation issues remain unresolved, and how and when the provisions will be implemented remains uncertain.

As a brief background, grandfathering was put into place to allow properties that are mapped into a higher-risk zone or in areas where the BFE increases to continue to use the current FIRM for future rating when the new FIRM becomes effective so long as the policyholder maintains the policy. Examples of affected map changes include buildings newly mapped into a high-risk area (e.g., Zone X to Zone A), mapped from a high- to higher-risk area (i.e., Zone A to Zone V), or whose BFE increases (for example, 12 feet above sea level to 14 feet above sea level).

Consider first structures that are newly mapped into high-risk zones. In 2010, FEMA created the PRP Eligibility Extension (EE) that allows for the low-cost PRP,[15] which was just for properties outside the high-risk area, to be written for any property that is newly mapped into a high-risk zone on or after October 1, 2008. Currently, the PRP EE continues to be available until Section 100207 of BW-12 is implemented. As of October 1, 2013, the premium for a PRP EE written on a building remapped into a high-risk zone is 19 percent higher than the premium for a PRP written outside high-risk zones.

PRP EE rating helps reduce the financial impact of map changes. For example, consider a single-family residence without a basement that is in a low-risk zone (Zone X) and qualifies for a $390 PRP for $200,000 in building coverage and $80,000 in contents coverage. Now assume that the flood map is updated and the home is in a high-risk zone (Zone AE) with the elevation of the lowest floor 1 foot below BFE. The premium on the home would rise to $5,090 without grandfathering. But, with PRP EE, the homeowner could purchase a PRP policy before the map change, which would convert to a PRP EE upon renewal and would be priced at $459.[16]

Now consider structures that are remapped from high-risk to higher-risk zones. Remapping a home from a Zone AE to Zone VE, even without any change in the home's elevation relative to BFE, can result in substantial premium increases. Grandfathering allows the homeowner to continue to pay the Zone AE rate or the rate corresponding to the current BFE. For example, $200,000 in building coverage and $80,000 in contents coverage runs $1,722 in Zone AE if the elevation of the single-family post-FIRM home is at BFE. If the home is remapped to Zone VE, the premium absent grandfathering rises to $7,094. With grandfathering, the premium remains at $1,722.[17]

Congress directed FEMA to phase in the premium increases due to flood-map changes over five years.[18] Thus, once FEMA implements the provisions of BW-12 related to grandfathering, premiums will increase annually by 20 percent of the difference between the rates required by the old and new maps. FEMA has determined that these phase-in provisions apply to post-FIRM properties and to pre-FIRM properties

---

[15] The NFIP's PRP offers lower-cost protection for businesses, homes, and apartments in areas of low to moderate flood risk. These areas outside of known floodplains are shown as B, C, or X zones on a FIRM. To be eligible for a PRP, a structure must also meet certain loss history requirements. For example, there cannot be three or more flood insurance claim payments for separate losses in any ten-year period or two claim payments for separate losses, each more than $1,000, in any ten-year period (FEMA, *Flood Insurance Manual, Effective October 1, 2013*, September 23, 2013d).

[16] The property must continue to meet the loss history requirements.

[17] This example is based on the October 2013 rates for a post-FIRM structure.

[18] Public Law 112-141, Moving Ahead for Progress in the 21st Century Act, July 6, 2012, Section 100207.

that are not receiving subsidized rates.[19] For pre-FIRM properties receiving subsidized rates, Section 100205 of BW-12 applies. Thus, pre-FIRM structures that were not continuously insured after July 6, 2012, will move directly to FEMA's estimate of the full-risk rate.[20] Some implementation issues remain to be resolved regarding the elimination of grandfathering. For example, it is unclear whether the five-year phase-in of new rates will apply to post-FIRM properties without an existing flood insurance policy or whether the phase-in will continue for properties sold during the phase-in period. Legislation has also been proposed to delay premium increases, prevent premium increases on previously grandfathered properties, and allow new owners of homes within high-risk areas to continue accessing the subsidized rates.[21] As a result, the ultimate impact of BW-12 may not be known for some time.

Examples of Premium Changes Due to Flood-Map Changes

We now provide some examples of how NFIP premiums may change with the adoption of a new FIRM that is similar to the PWM. We start with effects on pre-FIRM structures, which may be eligible for subsidized rates, and then turn to post-FIRM structures, which are not eligible for subsidized rates. We focus on the levels to which rates may ultimately rise, noting that the rate increases may be phased in over five years. The rate changes presented in the following tables assume that grandfathering has been eliminated, as is the intent of BW-12, even though FEMA has not yet issued the regulations that eliminate current grandfathering practices.

Pre-FIRM Structures

More than 85 percent of structures in the high-risk areas of the PWM are pre-FIRM structures. Table 4.7 provides figures on the number of one- to four-family pre-FIRM structures that fall in different categories relevant to determining rate changes due to map updates. Note that a substantial number of structures will be remapped from outside high-risk zones to inside high-risk zones, and the vast majority of these do not have flood insurance (see first row of Table 4.7).

We developed a range of cases to illustrate the potential effect of map changes on NFIP premiums paid by property owners in New York City. For a given structure elevation, the NFIP premium depends importantly on whether the building has a basement. (Recall that the NFIP offers only limited coverage for basements.) We thus generated scenarios with and without basements. We then developed plausible scenarios for structure elevation relative to BFE in the PWM. Structure elevation relative to BFE is a key determinant of many NFIP rates. The process for selecting the elevation scenarios is described in Appendix C.

---

[19] Recall that we use *pre-FIRM* to refer to construction date, not whether the structure receives a subsidized rate.

[20] Tom Hayes and Andy Neal, FEMA, personal communication, October 2013.

[21] See press release by Senator Mary Landrieu (Office of Senator Mary Landrieu, "Sen. Landrieu Introduces Flood Insurance Reform Legislation to Fix Biggert-Waters," press release, May 21, 2013).

Table 4.7
Remapping of Pre-FIRM One- to Four-Family Structures from the 2007 Flood Insurance Rate Map to the Preliminary Work Map

Zone Change Due to PWM	Insured as of October 2012	Not Insured as of October 2012	Total
Remapped from outside high-risk zones into high-risk zones	2,800	23,500	26,300
Remain in high-risk zones	11,600	7,500	19,100
All pre-FIRM structures	14,400	31,000	45,300

NOTE: Insurance status is based on the method used to calculate the upper bound for the take-up rate in Table 4.4. Numbers in this table have been rounded to the nearest hundred.

The scenarios are then used to develop examples, or cases, for how map changes may affect NFIP premiums. Although the cases examined may well be common once the new FIRM is issued, data are not currently available to predict the frequency with which the different cases would be expected to occur. In addition, premium increases greater and less than those shown in the examples provided will also likely occur.

Table 4.8 presents the different cases examined for pre-FIRM structures, first for structures with basements and then for structures without basements. In each case, the annual NFIP premium is calculated for $200,000 of building coverage and $80,000 of contents coverage. The deductible is $2,000 for building coverage and $2,000 for contents coverage for the pre-FIRM structures that receive pre-FIRM rates. The deductible is $1,000 for building coverage and $1,000 for contents coverage for PRP policies and for the pre-FIRM structures that receive post-FIRM rates.

For the substantial number of structures that will be remapped from outside the high-risk areas into the high-risk areas, the increase in NFIP premiums could be considerable. As shown in cases 1 through 3, a PRP is available for $429 outside the high-risk areas, and it would not be surprising to see NFIP premiums of $3,700 to $15,900 for the same structure once it is reclassified as being in a high-risk area.

Cases 4 through 7 apply to a pre-FIRM one- to four-family structure with basement that remains in the high-risk area. BW-12 retains the premium subsidy for primary residences currently in high-risk zones that were insured at the time the law was passed and maintain their insurance (for simplicity, we refer to such structures as *currently insured*). As shown in case 4, premiums on these structures will remain at $3,377. However, if a home is sold or if a homeowner lets his or her policy lapse, the premium will rise to unsubsidized rates (cases 5–7).[22]

Cases 8 through 12 repeat the analysis for pre-FIRM one- to four-family structures built on slabs. A different set of structure elevations is used for these cases (see the

---

[22] Note that the subsidized rate does not depend on structure elevation; however, once the policyholder starts paying the unsubsidized rate, structure elevation is required.

Table 4.8
Examples of Possible Changes in National Flood Insurance Program Annual Premium for a Primary One- to Four-Family, Pre-FIRM Home Due to Changes in the Flood Insurance Rate Map (for $200,000 in building coverage and $80,000 in contents coverage, assuming no grandfathering and full-rate phase-in)

	Current Situation			New Situation			
Case	Basement	Zone	Lowest Floor Relative to BFE (feet)[a]	Current Premium ($)	Zone	Lowest Floor Relative to BFE (feet)	New Premium ($)	Premium Change After Phase-In ($)
Structure with basement								
Remapped from outside high-risk zone to Zone AE								
1	Yes	X	—	429	AE	−5	4,100	3,671
2	Yes	X	—	429	AE	−9	8,045	7,616
3	Yes	X	—	429	AE	−13	16,291	15,862
Remains in Zone AE, primary residence, currently insured								
4	Yes	AE	—	3,377	AE	—	3,377	—
Remains in Zone AE currently not insured								
5	Yes	AE	—	—	AE	−5	4,100	—
6	Yes	AE	—	—	AE	−9	8,045	—
7	Yes	AE	—	—	AE	−13	16,291	—
Structure on slab (without basement)								
Remapped from outside high-risk zone to Zone AE								
8	No	X	—	390	AE	0	1,722	—
9	No	X	—	390	AE	−4	9,995	—

Table 4.8—Continued

| | Current Situation | | | | New Situation | | | |
| | Basement | Zone | Lowest Floor Relative to BFE (feet)[a] | Current Premium ($) | Zone | Lowest Floor Relative to BFE (feet) | New Premium ($) | Premium Change After Phase-In ($) |
Case								
Remains in Zone AE, primary residence, currently insured								
10	No	AE	—	2,922	AE	—	2,922	0
Remains in Zone AE, currently not insured								
11	No	AE	—	—	AE	0	1,722	−1,200
12	No	AE	—	—	AE	−4	9,995	7,073
Remapped from Zone AE to Zone VE, currently insured								
13	No	AE	—	2,922	VE	—	6,016	3,094
Remapped from Zone AE to Zone VE, currently not insured								
14	No	AE	—	—	VE	0	4,297	—
15	No	AE	—	—	VE	−4	23,244	—

SOURCE: Torrent Technologies' online flood insurance rating system.

NOTE: Based on rates set to take effect October 1, 2013. For pre-FIRM properties that received subsidized pre-FIRM rates, the deductibles are $2,000 for structure coverage and $2,000 for contents coverage. For PRP policies and pre-FIRM properties that receive the full-risk rates, the deductibles are $1,000 for structure coverage and $1,000 for contents coverage.

[a] Elevation is not required to set subsidized rates on pre-FIRM structures.

third column from the right) because these structures do not have basements that reach many feet underground. In addition, premium increases are included for structures on slabs that are remapped from Zone AE to Zone VE (cases 13–15). These scenarios are not reported for structures with basements because it seems less likely that structures with basements would have been built in the areas close to the beach that are now in VE zones.

Sizable premium increases are still observed in cases 8 through 12, although typically not as large as those for structures with basements. Very large premium increases are plausible for homes remapped from Zone AE to Zone VE. If the property owner maintains insurance, the rate will change from the subsidized Zone AE rate to the subsidized Zone VE rate (case 13). If, on the other hand, the structure is not currently insured, the property owner must pay the full-risk rate. A structure 1 foot above grade will pay $23,244 under the reasonable assumption that the difference between BFE in the PWM and ground level is 5 feet (resulting in a new elevation of –4) (case 15).

Post-FIRM Structures

Far fewer post-FIRM structures are affected by the proposed map changes than pre-FIRM structures. Table 4.9 reports the same information for post-FIRM structures that Table 4.7 did for pre-FIRM structures. Although Table 4.9 separates structures that are insured as of October 2012 from those that are not, it should be noted that current insurance status is not relevant to the pricing of post-FIRM properties.

To develop cases that illustrate the potential premium changes for post-FIRM properties, we started with data in the NFIP policy file on structure elevation for post-FIRM structures that had NFIP coverage as of October 2012 in the high-risk areas of the 2007 FIRM. That information was combined with a moderate range for the increase in BFE to generate a range of scenarios for structure elevation relative to BFE under the PWM. The process is described in Appendix C.

Table 4.10 provides examples of rate changes for post-FIRM structures. The table is similar in form to that for pre-FIRM structures (Table 4.8); however, current insur-

Table 4.9
Remapping of Post-FIRM One- to Four-Family Structures from the 2007 Flood Insurance Rate Map to Preliminary Work Map, by Insurance Status

Zone Change Due to PWM	Insured as of October 2012	Not Insured as of October 2012	Total
Remapped from outside high-risk zones to inside high-risk zones	400	2,100	2,500
Remain in high-risk zones	3,200	1,900	5,200
All post-FIRM structures	3,600	4,100	7,700

NOTE: Insurance status is based on the method used to calculate the upper bound for take-up rate in Table 4.4. Numbers in this table have been rounded to the nearest hundred.

Table 4.10
Examples of Possible Changes in National Flood Insurance Program Annual Premium for a Primary One- to Four-Family, Post-FIRM Home Due to Changes in the Flood Insurance Rate Map (for $200,000 in building coverage and $80,000 in contents coverage, assuming no grandfathering and full-rate phase-in)

	Current Situation					New Situation			Premium Change After Phase-In ($)
Case	Basement	Zone	Lowest Floor Relative to BFE (feet)	Current Pre-FIRM Premium ($)	Increase in BFE (feet)	Zone	Lowest Floor Relative to BFE (feet)	New Premium ($)	
Structure with basement									
Remapped from outside high-risk zone to Zone AE									
1	Yes	X	—	429[a]	—	AE	−1	2,365	1,936
2	Yes	X	—	429[a]	—	AE	−7	5,710	5,281
3	Yes	X	—	429[a]	—	AE	−9	8,045	7,616
Remains in Zone AE									
4	Yes	AE	3	506	2	AE	1	640	134
5	Yes	AE	−5	4,100	2	AE	−7	5,710	1,610
6	Yes	AE	3	506	4	AE	−1	2,365	1,859
7	Yes	AE	−5	4,100	4	AE	−9	8,045	3,945
Structure on slab (without basement)									
Remapped from outside high-risk zone to Zone AE									
8	No	X	—	390[a]	—	AE	2	601	211
9	No	X	—	390[a]	—	AE	0	1,722	1,332
10	No	X	—	390[a]	—	AE	−3	7,922	7,532

Table 4.10—Continued

		Current Situation				New Situation			
Case	Basement	Zone	Lowest Floor Relative to BFE FIRM (feet)	Current Pre-Premium ($)	Increase in BFE (feet)	Zone	Lowest Floor Relative to BFE (feet)	New Premium ($)	Premium Change After Phase-In ($)
Remains in Zone AE									
11	No	AE	4	487	2	AE	2	601	114
12	No	AE	−1	5,090	2	AE	−3	7,922	2,832
13	No	AE	4	487	4	AE	0	1,723	1,236
14	No	AE	−1	5,090	4	AE	−5	12,296	7,206
Remapped from Zone AE to Zone VE									
15	No	AE	4	487	2	VE	2	6,456	5,969
16	No	AE	−1	5,090	2	VE	−3	19,107	14,017
17	No	AE	4	487	4	VE	0	8,706	8,219
18	No	AE	−1	5,090	4	VE	−5	27,460	22,370

SOURCE: Torrent Technologies' online flood insurance rating system.

NOTE: Based on rates set to take effect October 1, 2013. The deductibles are $1,000 for structure coverage and $1,000 for contents coverage.

a Elevation is not required to set PRP premium.

ance status does not affect rates on post-FIRM structures, and no distinction is made between structures that are currently insured and those that are not.

Cases 1 through 3 illustrate that premium increases can be substantial for post-FIRM structures with basements that are remapped from outside the high-risk areas into high-risk areas. Because these structures were outside the high-risk zones when constructed, it would not be surprising to see structures with large negative elevations under the new FIRM. As can be seen, cases in which premiums rise by $2,000 to $7,500 would not be surprising.

The building codes required by the NFIP prohibit structures with basements to be built in high-risk zones (the resulting structure elevation would be below BFE). Thus, one might not expect a substantial number of post-FIRM structures with basements in the high-risk zones of the 2007 FIRM (cases 4–7). However, the NFIP policy file suggests that some of these structures have basements, but further investigation of the quality of the data is necessary before conclusions about the frequency of basements can be made. The 2- to 4-foot increase in BFE that is typical in the PWM means that NFIP premiums could increase substantially for many of these structures. For example, a structure with a basement that is 5 feet below BFE under the current FIRM could easily end up at 9 feet below BFE in the updated FIRM, with premiums increasing from $4,100 to $8,045 (case 7).

Cases 8 through 14 repeat the analysis for post-FIRM one- to four-family structures built on slabs. The structure elevations in these cases reflect the observed elevations of post-FIRM structures without basements that had NFIP policies in October 2012. The premiums and premium increases for these cases are similar to those for the structures with basements.

Very large increases could be observed for structures remapped from Zone AE to Zone VE (cases 15–18). A structure in Zone AE of the current FIRM that is 1 foot below BFE pays a premium of $5,090. However, if BFE increases by 4 feet and the area is remapped as Zone VE, the premium would increase to $27,460 (case 18).

Impact of the Flood Insurance Rate Map Changes on Private Flood Rates

According to our interviews, private insurers seem to be responding differently to the information that the PWM (and the advisory maps that preceded it) provide. Some are advising their clients that, if they need to rebuild, they should rebuild to the BFE in the PWM. Other private insurers are not insisting on that requirement or adjusting their pricing until the map is adopted in final form, which could take years. Some private insurers of flood have their own engineers and risk modelers and are continuously adjusting their pricing accordingly. Because these carriers do not rely solely on the FIRM to rate policies, a change in the FIRM may not significantly affect their pricing structure because they may have already adjusted prices for changes in catastrophic risk (this is discussed in more detail in Chapter Three).

CHAPTER FIVE

The Effects of Higher Flood Insurance Premiums on the Housing Market

Chapter Four shows that the elimination of NFIP subsidies and updates in the FIRM to more accurately reflect risk may lead to large increases in flood insurance premiums for households in New York City. The increases will depend on the location and characteristics of the structure and, in some cases, whether there is flood insurance already in place. The increases will also depend on decisions FEMA has yet to make on implementing BW-12. In this chapter, we examine how the rate changes might affect different categories of households. More specifically, we examine potential impacts on

- households in owner-occupied housing units
- renters of residential housing units
- landlords.

For each, we discuss what economic reasoning would lead us to expect in terms of the direction and incidence of the effects. When possible, we also provide demographic information on the population affected. The increase in flood insurance premiums may also have important impacts on the businesses in high-risk areas—some of which rent their space and others that own it. Because the percentage of businesses with NFIP coverage is quite small, we do not discuss the impacts here but leave that discussion for future work.

Households in Owner-Occupied Housing Units

First consider a household that owns and occupies a single-family home. Assume that there is a mortgage on the home and that the MPR requires the homeowner to carry $250,000 in coverage. Finally, assume that, as a result of flood-map changes, the annual flood insurance premium rises by $5,000. Standard economic reasoning would argue that the increase in the flood insurance premium would be capitalized in the value of the property. If we assume a typical discount rate of 5 percent, the price of the property would fall $100,000.[1] Thus, one might expect the price of a $500,000 home (which is not unusual in the Rockaway area) to fall 20 percent to $400,000. When flood insurance premiums increase, the homeowner should expect a drop in property value, as well as the higher annual insurance payment.[2]

Several studies have investigated whether such changes occur in practice. Bin, Kruse, and Landry find that the difference in property value, other factors held constant, is roughly equal to the difference in the capitalized value of flood insurance premiums.[3] In that study, the authors examined home prices in Carteret County, North Carolina, comparing prices of homes located in the floodplain with prices of similar homes outside the floodplain. Harrison, Smersh, and Schwartz did a similar study on property transactions in Alachua County, Florida.[4] In contrast to the findings of Bin, Kruse, and Landry, they find that the reduction in property value due to the increase in insurance premium payments is less than the capitalized premium, although they show that the reduction is closer to the capitalized premium in the more-recent periods covered by their data.[5]

The premium-increase example presented here assumes that the property owner must purchase flood insurance. The effect of increased premiums might be less on structures for which the purchase of flood insurance is voluntary.[6] However, even if flood insurance is voluntary, when deciding what they would be willing to pay for the property, prospective buyers may take into account the higher risk signaled by the increase in flood insurance premium. The effect may also occur in advance of an expected premium increase. For example, a prospective buyer of a property in the PWM may offer a discounted price based on the knowledge that he or she will have to pay high flood insurance premiums very soon and then into the future.

The premium increases illustrated in Chapter Four may pose an economic hardship to many households. Table 5.1 provides an overview of the population living in

---

[1] The discounted sum of an infinite series of $5,000 annual payments is

$$\frac{\$5,000}{0.05}.$$

[2] Property value is determined by a variety of factors, and it is possible that property value could rise even when flood insurance premiums increase, even if not as much as it would have risen without the premium increase. Also, these changes in property value assume that prospective buyers are aware of the MPR and the premium.

[3] Okmyung Bin, Jamie Brown Kruse, and Craig E. Landry, "Flood Hazards, Insurance Rates, and Amenities: Evidence from the Coastal Housing Market," *Journal of Risk and Insurance*, Vol. 75, No. 1, March 2008, pp. 63–82.

[4] David M. Harrison, Greg T. Smersh, and Arthur L. Schwartz, Jr., "Environmental Determinants of Housing Prices: The Impact of Flood Zone Status," *Journal of Real Estate Research*, Vol. 21, No. 1–2, 2001, pp. 3–20.

[5] Harrison, Smersh, and Schwartz, 2001.

[6] Recall that flood insurance is voluntary for properties without mortgages that are in the 100-year floodplain.

the high-risk areas of the PWM and, for comparison, of the population in the high-risk areas of the 2007 FIRM and all New York City.[7] As can be seen from the table, approximately 5 percent of New York City residents, households, and housing units are in the high-risk area of the PWM, and population demographics in the high-risk areas are similar to those of New York City as a whole. One-third of all housing units in the high-risk area of the PWM are owner-occupied (see "Occupancy status" portion of Table 5.1), and we suspect that the owner-occupied rate is much higher for one- to four-family homes.

The median income of households living in owner-occupied housing units in the high-risk areas of the PWM is approximately $100,000, and 37 percent of households living in owner-occupied housing units in the PWM have incomes less than $75,000.[8] Premium increases of $5,000 to $10,000 were not unusual in the examples presented in Chapter Four, which amounts to 5–10 percent of median household income. The percentage of median income is even higher when one considers the full premium rather than just the increase from an initial level. For comparison, national census data show that, on average, households in owner-occupied housing units spend 1.8 percent of their annual pretax income on home insurance, maintenance, repair, and other housing expenses, excluding mortgage payments and property taxes.[9] The census figures include households that do not live in high-risk areas, so one would expect the percentage spent on insurance to be lower than in the high-risk areas of New York City. However, these figures lend perspective to the premium increases and final premium levels that could occur in New York City. A more complete analysis of the impact of NFIP rates should consider the magnitude of the increases relative to household wealth. However, such wealth data are not readily available for the households in the New York City high-risk areas.

The increase in NFIP rates could have several negative consequences for the households and communities in high-risk areas. Large increases in insurance premiums may make it infeasible for current homeowners to stay in their homes. In addition, the drop in property value may cause the mortgage balance to be greater than the property value in some cases, giving homeowners an incentive to walk away from their homes. The result could be substantial population turnover in communities subject to large rate

---

[7] The statistics are based on census data at the block-group or census-tract level. The census block groups and tracks were overlaid on the flood-zone map, and population and housing units allocated to the high-risk areas based on whether the centroid of the block-group or census-tract area is in the high-risk area. Lower error is expected when block-group data are used.

[8] For comparison, note that New York City defines *low-income households* as households with incomes less than or equal to 80 percent of area median income (AMI). The low-income threshold in New York City is $48,100 for a one-person household and $68,700 for a four-person household. The income cutoffs in Table 5.1 are based on the categories reported by the census.

[9] U.S. Bureau of Labor Statistics, "Consumer Expenditures in 2009," news release, USDL-10-1390, October 2010.

Table 5.1
Population Demographics in New York City and the High-Risk Flood Zones

Characteristic	New York City	High-Risk Zones of 2007 FIRM	High-Risk Zones of PWM[a]
Population	8,078,471	233,489	429,957
Households	3,047,249	93,057	165,757
Housing units (both occupied and unoccupied)	3,343,424	101,774	181,195
Age (% of population)			
≤17 years	22	21	21
18 to 69 years	69	67	68
70+ years	8	12	11
Race (% of population)			
White	44	53	55
Black	25	25	26
Asian	13	10	10
Other	18	12	10
Households below poverty line (%)[b]	18	21	18
Education (% of population greater than 25 years old)			
Less than high school degree	21	21	20
High school degree	26	26	27
Some college	20	20	21
Bachelor's degree or above	33	34	32
Occupancy status (% of housing units)			
Owner-occupied	30	25	33
Renter-occupied	61	67	59
Unoccupied	9	9	9
Mortgage status for owner-occupied housing units (% of owner-occupied housing units)			
Has a mortgage	64	62	64
Does not have a mortgage	36	38	36
Annual income of households living in owner-occupied housing units (%)			
<$25,000	13	7	7
$25,000 to $50,000	17	16	16
$50,000 to $75,000	17	13	14

Table 5.1—Continued

Characteristic	New York City	High-Risk Zones of 2007 FIRM	High-Risk Zones of PWM[a]
$75,000 to $100,000	15	12	13
$100,000 to $150,000	19	18	19
≥$150,000	20	35	31
Annual income of households living in rental housing units (%)			
<$25,000	36	33	32
$25,000 to $50,000	25	20	21
$50,000 to $75,000	16	14	15
$75,000 to $100,000	9	10	10
$100,000 to $150,000	8	10	10
≥$150,000	7	13	12
Household size of households living in owner-occupied housing units (%)			
1	25	24	22
2	29	30	30
3	17	18	18
4	16	14	17
≥5	14	12	13
Household size of households living in rental housing units (%)			
1	36	39	39
2	27	30	30
3	16	14	15
4	11	9	9
≥5	9	7	7

SOURCE: U.S. Census Bureau, American Community Survey, 2006–2010. The statistics on mortgage status for owner-occupied housing units and income of households living in owner-occupied units are based on census-tract data. The remaining statistics in the table are based on block-group data.

NOTE: Because of rounding, percentages do not always sum to 100.

[a] Excludes areas subject to high flood risk due to riverine flooding. These areas are expected to increase the area in the high-risk zones of the PWM by less than 10 percent.

[b] In 2012, the poverty guideline for a one-person household was $11,170 and, for a four-person household, $23,040 (Office of the Assistant Secretary for Planning and Evaluation, U.S. Department of Health and Human Services, "2012 HHS Poverty Guidelines," last updated February 9, 2012).

hikes, foreclosures, homes that are vacant for some period of time, and short sales.[10] Lower property values would also affect New York City tax revenue, absent compensating changes in tax rates. Although significant negative impacts are plausible, further analysis is needed to characterize what effects will occur in practice and in what areas. In particular, more information is needed on the distribution of the actual premium changes that will occur in the high-risk areas and the incomes and wealth of the households affected. Again, exactly what those premium changes will be and exactly when they might take effect—particularly for pre-FIRM structures and properties subject to grandfathering—will depend on how FEMA implements certain provisions of BW-12.

Renters of Residential Housing Units

Renters account for approximately two-thirds of the households living in the high-risk areas of the new PWM, with a large fraction living in multifamily and mixed-use dwellings. The economics of the rental market, combined with rent control and stabilization policies in New York City, will influence how increased flood insurance rates paid by landlords will affect renters.

Premium increases are likely to have little short-run impact on rents. In the short run, the supply of housing units is fixed, and the demand for rental housing in the high-risk areas will likely not shift as a result of premium increases faced by landlords.[11] Thus, the price at which demand and supply balance would not change. Over the longer run, markets will adjust to the higher costs, with rents possibly increasing. The size of the increases will depend on the elasticity of demand, as well as the response on the supply side of the market. For example, increased flood premiums could reduce the profitability of rental housing, reducing the investment in new units or the maintenance and refurbishing of existing units. As a result, the supply of rental housing in the high-risk areas could fall, leading to an increase in rents. However, even if the supply of rental housing falls, the increase in rates might be minimal if the demand for rental housing is very sensitive to price—for example, if other sources of comparable rental housing are readily available outside the high-risk areas.

Further work is needed to characterize both the demand and supply sides of the rental market in the high-risk areas. Different outcomes are plausible on the supply side of the market. Under some scenarios, the major adjustment might be a decline in the land value for rental properties, analogous to the expectation for owner-occupied housing units. In that case, there could be little change in rents, even over the long run. Under other scenarios, as discussed above, the increase in flood insurance premiums could eventually reduce the rental housing stock and increase rents. Also part of the

---

[10] A property could remain vacant while it goes through the foreclosure process—specifically, after the property owner moves out and while the bank is processing the home for resale.

[11] The demand curve would indicate the relationship between the amount of rental housing demanded and its price (the rent).

calculation would be the rent control and stabilization policies in New York, which limit how much rents can increase.[12] How those policies allow for adjustments due to sharp increases in insurance costs would need to be further investigated.

Any significant rent increases that do occur could have adverse effects on the renter population. As shown in Table 5.1, approximately one-third of households living in rental units in New York City's high-risk areas earn less than $25,000 per year. Rent increases could lead to reductions in the low-income households living in the high-risk areas of the PWM, and perhaps reduce the availability of low-income housing in New York City overall. Again, the actual change in the insurance premiums for rental structures and how those increases would affect renters needs to be better understood before predictions on outcomes can be made.

Landlords

The preceding discussion on renters suggests that landlords will bear the burden of increased flood premiums in the short run. Existing landlords may also see their property values decline. Lower profits, or losses, on current operations, could lead some landlords to sell properties, although there could be little change in the rental operations of the new firms. Lower property values could result in lower city tax revenue.

---

[12] U.S. Statute 61-193, Housing and Rent Act of 1947, June 30, 1947; New York City Rent Stabilization Law of 1969 (codified in New York City Administrative Code §§ 26-501–26-520).

CHAPTER SIX

Issues to Consider in Responding to Insurance Premium Increases

The analysis in the preceding chapters has shown that many New Yorkers will face substantially higher flood insurance premiums moving forward. Many more structures will be in areas considered high-risk than in the past, and premiums for many structures already in high-risk areas will be based on considerably higher flood levels. These changes are caused by updates of the FEMA-issued FIRM for the city, changes in BW-12 that remove many of the subsidies embedded in the NFIP, and a general understanding that flood risk is greater in New York City than previously thought. We have also documented gaps in the flood insurance coverage held by New Yorkers. It is important to note that these gaps are driven by the substantial number of households and businesses that do not purchase the coverage that is available (even though often required by federal law). It is also driven by the lack of availability of certain types of coverage, such as coverage for business interruption attributable to flood.

These substantial premium increases will reduce the disposable income or wealth (or both) of many households and may well be unaffordable for some. In the absence of intervention, the consequence may be foreclosures, turnover, and hardship for some of New York City's more-vulnerable citizens. And, with sea-level rise, the situation may only deteriorate over time because of increasing risk and increasing risk-based rates. Although the higher flood insurance premiums have clear negative effects for some New Yorkers, there are also benefits to moving to flood insurance premiums that more accurately reflect risk. The risk-based premiums can create incentives for property owners and government planners to take appropriate measures to reduce risk. They also put the cost of living in high-risk areas on those who own property in those areas, as opposed to on taxpayers in non–high-risk areas who may be called on to pay rebuilding costs or cover the costs of subsidized premiums.

In this concluding chapter, we discuss issues to consider in responding to the substantial increase in flood insurance premiums. We first discuss risk mitigation and then address affordability.

Risk Mitigation

The obvious way to reduce risk-based insurance premiums is to reduce risk. Risk-mitigation measures can be considered at many different scales. Coastal protection projects, such as dunes, bulkheads, or multipurpose levees, can reduce storm surge. However, these projects would be implemented over years or decades and therefore will not reduce the short- to medium-term impact of flooding risk or rising insurance premiums for city residents. Individual buildings can be retrofitted to reduce loss in the event flooding does occur. For example, elevating or flood-proofing the structure reduces the likelihood that floodwater will enter a structure. Installing vents that allow water to pass through, moving electrical equipment, and other measures can reduce damage when water does enter a building.

New York City is actively considering a range of options at all different scales.[1] Newly constructed and substantially improved buildings are required to be built to standards that reduce the risks of damage from flooding. But because the floodplain in New York City is largely developed, creating strategies for risk mitigation for the existing building stock will be important. The particular characteristics of the older building stock in the dense, urban environment of New York City pose challenges to applying typical risk-mitigation approaches that are often effective elsewhere. For example, an analysis by the New York City Mayor's Office found that 39 percent of buildings in the high-risk zones of the PWM would be difficult to elevate because they are on narrow lots or attached or semi-attached buildings.[2] It is thus important to continue to search for innovative ways to reduce flood risk that are tailored to dense urban environments like New York City.

Several issues should be considered in developing strategies for mitigating flood risk in New York City. First, it will be necessary to better understand what premium increases will actually occur. To do this, more information is needed on the flood insurance premiums that the NFIP will charge. In Chapter Four, we developed plausible examples of how rates might change, but we did not have the data to determine how frequently various scenarios would occur. The most important piece of missing information is the elevation of structures in the high-risk areas of the PWM. Structure elevation relative to BFE is currently available for relatively few structures in the high-risk areas of the PWM, and the reliability of available data on basements needs to be evaluated.[3] In the absence of this information, New York City will need either proxies or estimations of the figures. These could be based on statistical sampling of actual

---

[1]   City of New York, 2013.

[2]   City of New York, 2013, p. 99.

[3]   Structure elevations are currently available for post-FIRM properties with NFIP coverage in the high-risk areas. These elevations are required in the policy application process. The problem is that, as shown in Table 2.8 in Chapter Two, there are only 3,183 of these policies. Data on past policies might be able to increase the number somewhat.

building elevations. Better information on structure elevations would allow better estimates of how coastal protection projects would reduce risk and flood insurance premiums. It would also inform analyses of how many property owners are facing very high insurance premiums and what risk-mitigation strategies at the building level might be appropriate to reduce the risk of flooding.

A risk-mitigation strategy should jointly consider measures at all different scales. Risk-mitigation decisions made in isolation can result in poor decisions. For example, it most likely would not make sense to elevate individual structures if a levee is going to reduce BFE, even if the levee is not completed for a decade. Not only is it important for government planners to adopt a holistic approach, but property owners also need to be well informed about the overall approach. In order to make good risk-mitigation investments, they need to know what flood levels in their area will look like in the future.[4]

This holistic approach will likely result in a multilayered strategy for reducing flood risk. A suite of mitigation tools and incentives should be considered based on specific physical and socioeconomic attributes of New York City neighborhoods. These might include low-interest loans or grants to individuals to fund mitigation efforts or larger-scale coastal protection measures to fortify whole neighborhoods. They might also include changes in land use that remove structures from some areas when property owners are willing to sell.

In terms of building-level risk-mitigation measures, it is important that city staff work with FEMA to make sure that such risk-mitigation measures are appropriately reflected in NFIP premiums. Premium reductions for mitigation measures are often not readily available in NFIP rate tables. Rather, the policy must go through the NFIP's "submit-for-rate" process. This means that the insurance agent must submit the policy to the insurer administering the NFIP policy or to FEMA to determine the rate, rather than quickly pull it off a rate table. Submitting a policy for rating can cause delay and may depend on subjective assessments. Consequently, it currently is not easy for building owners to quickly determine the return on investment in mitigation measures in terms of lower premiums. There is much to be gained by New York City working with FEMA to establish a schedule of premium reductions (or at least the range of premium reductions) for different mitigation measures and publicly disseminating the information.

Finally, strategies should be considered for increasing awareness of flood risk and the percentage of homes and small businesses with flood insurance in the high-risk areas. Although doing so does not reduce risk directly, it can create an incentive to

---

[4]   The source of funding for these projects, whether local, state, or federal, is also of clear importance. Assessment of options for different funding sources and the advantages and disadvantages of each is beyond the scope of this analysis.

reduce risk, although how people respond to these incentives is not well understood.[5] It also ensures that resources are available to rebuild and recover following a large flood event. In Chapters Two and Four, we showed that only 55 percent of one- to four-family homes in the high-risk areas of the 2007 FIRM have flood insurance and that tens of thousands of homes and businesses will soon be added to high-risk zones that do not currently have insurance. Many businesses and residents that will be in the expanded high-risk areas may not be aware of their flood risk. Strategies, such as educational campaigns, can be considered to increase awareness of flood risk and the notoriously low take-up rates among property owners who are not required to buy flood insurance. Programs to improve enforcement of the MPR can also be considered. New York City should work with FEMA and the New York State Department of Financial Services to explore programs in these areas.

Affordability

Analysis of the costs and benefits of various mitigation approaches is an appropriate way to make decisions at both the societal and individual levels on what actions to take. However, such analysis does not necessarily address the distribution of costs and benefits across households and businesses. Congress recognized the challenge of affordability that would be imposed by BW-12. It required that the NFIP study "methods of establishing an affordability framework" and that the National Academy of Sciences conduct an analysis of a means-tested voucher program.[6] Despite this, no guidance was provided on how local, state, or federal agencies could address affordability issues and the potential impacts of the legislation on businesses, individuals, and neighborhoods. The reports, even once produced, will not necessarily address the unique concerns of major metropolitan areas, such as New York City, so it is important for New York City to understand how various policy options would affect its residents and businesses.[7] In this section, we provide examples of the types of proposals that have been made to

---

[5]   See, for example, Wharton Risk Management and Decision Processes Center, *Managing Large-Scale Risk in a New Era of Catastrophes: Insuring, Mitigating and Financing Recovery from Natural Disasters in the United States*, March 2008, Chapter 12, which describes the various perceptual biases and other factors that can cause people to underinvest in mitigation. Even when flood insurance is mandatory and a household buys an expensive policy, such factors as lack of access to credit or unsure reduction in the flood insurance premium may prevent investment in mitigation measures.

[6]   BW-12, Section 100206. Such a program would provide a voucher that could be used for the purchase of an NFIP policy and would be available to households with incomes or assets below a certain level.

[7]   At the time of this writing (October 2013), the National Research Council is about to begin the study, with completion of phase 1 set for late 2014 (National Research Council, Water Science and Technology Board, Division on Earth and Life Studies, "New Study Announcement: Analysis of Costs and Benefits of Reforms to the National Flood Insurance Program—Phase 1," undated).

address affordability and identify the type of information needed to better assess these options.

Options for Addressing Affordability

A variety of approaches have been proposed for addressing the affordability issue. Providing assistance to NFIP policyholders based on financial need could help reduce the financial impact of an increase in flood insurance premiums. As GAO points out, this type of assistance could take several forms, including tax credits, grants, and vouchers that could be applied toward the cost of flood insurance.[8] A major concern about this type of intervention is that it distorts the price signal that incentivizes property owners to invest in risk-mitigation measures in order to reduce premiums. For example, a voucher that reduces the cost of insurance from $5,000 to $1,000 per year would limit the premium reductions the property owner would realize from risk-reduction measures. Kousky and Kunreuther have developed a proposal that addresses this incentive issue. They propose a means-tested voucher program coupled with a requirement that mitigation measures be taken that make sense for the property.[9]

Proposals have also been made to allow higher deductibles on NFIP policies and then establish a public program to pay part of the deductible for lower-income households should an event occur.[10] The actuarial costs of a policy are a function of the deductible, the limit, and the risk of an event. By increasing the deductible above the $5,000 limit currently allowed on residential properties, the premium for flood insurance can be reduced significantly.[11] As a consequence, households have, in effect, less insurance, but the deductible-sharing program covers part of the loss when an event occurs. Again, the effects on risk-mitigation incentives would need to be considered. Also to be considered is whether households that are not eligible for the deductible cost-sharing program would indeed be able to pay the deductible they select should an event occur.

Programs have also been considered that provide subsidized loans or grants for risk-mitigation measures for low-income households. The goal would be to reduce flood risks and thereby reduce flood insurance premiums for these households. Again, the city would need to work with the NFIP to develop a set of risk-mitigation measures

---

[8]   GAO, 2013, p. 35.

[9]   Carolyn Kousky and Howard Kunreuther, "Addressing Affordability in the National Flood Insurance Program," Washington, D.C.: Resources for the Future and the Wharton Risk Management and Decision Processes Center, Issue Brief 13-02, August 2013, p. 2.

[10]   The New York City Mayor's Office recommended further study of this approach in its 2013 report on building a more resilient New York (City of New York, 2013, p. 102).

[11]   Increasing deductibles for flood insurance has a large effect on the expected payout on a policy (and thus the required premium) because most flood claims are small (see Table 3.2 in Chapter Three for NFIP claims due to Hurricane Sandy).

that would be both relevant for the building stock in New York City and eligible for premium credit from the NFIP.

Assessing Affordability Options

More information is needed to address the advantages and disadvantages of alternative strategies for addressing affordability. As for the analysis of mitigation strategies, better information is needed on what the NFIP premiums will be on the structures in New York City. Also, more information is needed on the relationship between NFIP premiums and household income. We examined the income distribution for all households in the high-risk areas in Chapter Five, but premiums may vary considerably throughout the high-risk areas, and household incomes in the areas most affected need to be considered at a much greater level of detail. Such analysis would improve understanding of the scope of the problem by identifying specific neighborhoods that will be facing steep premium increases and the number of households that would qualify for various types of assistance.

In Conclusion

The threats posed by rising sea levels and extreme weather events are real, and it is just a matter of time before another catastrophic storm strikes the eastern seaboard. But if the city takes steps to mitigate the risk of flood damage and increase flood insurance coverage for its residents and businesses, it will promote greater resilience and faster recovery in response to future storms. It is important for the city to continue to collect the required data and conduct the studies to determine what packages of mitigation and affordability programs make sense. This process and the resulting programs can, in turn, provide useful guidance for other regions that find themselves in similar situations.

Background on Flood Insurance

This appendix provides background on the types of insurance available to homeowners and businesses in New York City. There is a discussion of general insurance coverage types, but the focus is on flood insurance because Hurricane Sandy was primarily a flood event and the lack of flood insurance was one of the major gaps observed after the storm. The appendix begins by discussing residential insurance, which includes a discussion of homeowner's and renter's insurance; the Coastal Market Assistance Program (C-MAP), which is a lender of last resort of homeowner's insurance for coastal properties; and the NFIP, the primary provider of flood insurance for homeowners. This is followed by a discussion of commercial insurance, how different sizes of firms buy insurance differently, and some of the deviations in flood insurance coverage provided by the private market from that provided through the NFIP.

Residential Insurance

Homeowner's Policies

The basic insurance policy in New York is based on the historical New York Fire Policy. The New York Fire Policy cannot be amended, but most insurers have added to that the standard homeowner's policy (HO-3) developed by the Insurance Services Organization. Five different types of policies are available that offer varied coverage for one- and two-family homes, but the HO-3 policy is the most widely held type of insurance for New York residents. According to our interviews, uptake of homeowner's insurance in New York City is estimated at 96 percent to 99 percent. This is in line with the U.S. Census Bureau's 2011 New York City and Housing and Vacancy Survey, which estimates that 95 percent of homeowners have insurance.

Coverage Types

The basic homeowner's policy tends to wrap four coverage types (fire, windstorm, theft, and liability) into one policy, though standard policies tend to include other perils, as is discussed below. The amount of coverage available for personal property and other losses is typically a percentage of the insured value of the home.

Table A.1
Standard Coverage Amounts for Residential Personal Property

Coverage	Percentage of Insured Value
Garages, sheds, etc.	10
Personal property on premises	50
Personal property off premises	10 (or $1,000, whichever is greater)
Additional living expenses	20

SOURCE: New York State Department of Financial Services, "Homeowners Resource Center," updated April 8, 2013.

Perils

Natural perils covered by standard residential homeowner's policy include the following:

- fire
- windstorm
- hail
- explosion (except from boilers).

Perils excluded under standard homeowner's insurance policies are the following:

- flood
- earthquake
- war
- nuclear accident.

Insurance providers also sell additional protection that includes personal possessions but has the same peril exclusions listed above. They also sell renter's insurance to cover possessions and personal liability of nonhomeowners. Renter's insurance is discussed separately.

Deductibles

Standard deductibles can range between $250 and $7,500. In our interviews with insurance industry professionals, we heard that the most-common deductibles are $500 or $1,000, with about 50 percent of people choosing the $500 deductible and 50 percent choosing the $1,000 deductible.

Hurricane deductibles are separate from the standard deductible and are typically triggered by the wind speed and when the damage occurred. Different insurers choose different triggers. Some deductibles are triggered when wind speeds reach 74 mph (a category 1 hurricane) and others when wind speeds reach 100 mph (a category 2 hurricane). The deductible applies when a loss occurs 12 hours (or 24 hours for some insurers) before or after an official warning has been issued by the National Weather

Service (NWS). Deductible amounts for New York City are typically 5 percent of the insured value but can vary by carrier (see Table A.2). Hurricane deductibles did not

Table A.2
New York State Hurricane Deductibles for Insurers with the Largest Number of Claims from Hurricane Sandy

Company Name	Number of Claims	Percentage of All Claims	Hurricane Deductible[a]	Trigger[b]
Allstate Insurance Group	81,679	21	5% of insured value	100 mph winds anywhere in the state (within 24 hours before to 12 hours after NWS declaration)
State Farm	55,759	14	5% of insured value	74 mph winds anywhere in the same county (within 12 hours before to 12 hours after NWS declaration)
Travelers Group	41,721	11	$1,000 for category 1; 5% of insured value for category 2 or higher	Hurricane declaration by NWS in any coastal county
Berkshire Hathaway (GEICO)	34,102	9	Not available	Not available
Liberty Mutual Group	32,856	8	5% of insured value	100 mph winds anywhere in the state (within 12 hours before to 12 hours after NWS declaration)
Metropolitan Group	21,537	6	3% (Bronx, New York, and Richmond counties) 5% (Kings, Queens)	74 mph winds anywhere in the state (within 12 hours before to 12 hours after NWS declaration)
Tower Group	16,835	4	5% of insured value	Hurricane declaration by NWS anywhere in the state (within 12 hours before and 12 hours after)
Nationwide Group	15,584	4	5% of insured value	Hurricane declaration by NWS anywhere in the state or a contiguous state

Table A.2—Continued

Company Name	Number of Claims	Percentage of All Claims	Hurricane Deductible[a]	Trigger[b]
Hartford Fire and Casualty Group	14,740	4	5% if within 2 miles of coast or 2% elsewhere	100 mph winds anywhere in the state (12 hours before to 12 hours after)
USAA Group	11,636	3	$2,000 if insured value is <$100,000; 2% if insured value is >$100,000	Hurricane declared by NWS in any coastal county in the state (within 12 hours before to 12 hours after)
Narragansett Bay Insurance Company	11,056	3	Not available	Not available
New York Property Insurance Underwriting Association	10,720	3	Not available	Not available

[a] Information on the hurricane deductibles was extracted from New York State Department of Financial Services, 2013a.

[b] 74 mph winds represent a category 1 hurricane. 100 mph winds represent a category 2 hurricane. Hurricane deductibles did not apply during Hurricane Sandy because wind speeds dropped below hurricane strength shortly before making landfall in New York and New Jersey.

apply during Hurricane Sandy because wind speeds dropped below hurricane strength shortly before making landfall in New York and New Jersey.

Loss Evaluation

Replacement Cost

Standard homeowner's insurance coverage is based on the replacement cost of the home, which is estimated by the insurance company. Insurers often sell additional optional coverage, such as an additional 25 percent of the coverage limit. Additionally, some insurers include 10-percent coverage A for building ordinance or law in the homeowner's policy with an option to purchase additional coverage for bringing the building up to code if building codes have significantly changed since the house was initially insured.

Select Value

Select value refers to insurance coverage that is based on a chosen value that is less than the replacement cost. If the select value is less than 80 percent of the replacement value, this option can affect how the homeowner is paid in the event of a claim. The insurer will pay the greater of the actual cash value of what was damaged or the proportion of the cost of the repair relative to the percentage of insurance to replacement cost.[1]

Renter's Policies

New York building owners who rent to residents are required by law to maintain insurance on the domicile. This insurance covers the building, and the owners can file claims for damages to the building structure. However, the landlord's building insurance does not cover tenants' personal property. The landlord is responsible for tenants' personal property damages only if the landlord knows about a hazardous condition and fails to fix it in a reasonable time frame.[2]

In most cases, a landlord's insurance does not cover a tenant's personal property. Thus, tenants are liable for their own property damages and losses. Renters face the additional risk of paying for injuries sustained on their rented property. If a person is injured while on a renter's premises, the renter could potentially be held liable for the injured person's medical expenses.

Coverage Types

Basic renter's insurance generally covers personal property, loss of use, personal liability, and medical payments to others in the event of an injury in the tenant's residence. Property that is damaged or destroyed by a covered cause is also usually covered by renter's insurance. This property includes electronics, clothes, furniture, sports equipment, appliances, jewelry, and collectibles.

Renter's insurance usually covers costs associated with loss or damage caused by fire; smoke; theft; vandalism; hail; windstorms; lightning; explosions; falling objects; weight of snow, ice, or sleet; electrical surges; and water from plumbing failure, appliance failure, fire sprinklers, or other accidental discharges of water.[3] However, basic renter's insurance does not cover flood damage.

In terms of liability for other people's property, damages, and costs, renter's insurance usually covers injuries that others incur while at the renter's home. This includes medical expenses and any resulting lawsuits (generally up to a $100,000 limit[4]). Renter's insurance also usually covers liability for damage that the renter may cause to other people's property and the renter's living expenses if the rental unit is damaged and the

---

[1] Information on select value is interpreted from New York State Department of Financial Services (*New York State Homeowners Coverage: Approved Independent Mandatory Hurricane Deductibles: Revised as of 3/20/2013*, March 2013a) and our discussions with insurance professionals.

[2] New York State Department of Financial Services, "Homeowners and Tenants Insurance," undated; referenced April 10, 2013.

[3] New York State Department of Financial Services, undated.

[4] Susan Stellin, "A Word to the Wise Renter: Insurance," *New York Times*, January 27, 2012.

renter needs to live elsewhere during the repair.[5] This additional living expense (ALE) coverage applies only to covered perils; so, if a tenant cannot live in his or her apartment because of flood or loss of electricity, a common occurrence during Hurricane Sandy, the tenant is not eligible for ALE. Some policies allow for two weeks of ALE coverage if a renter cannot live in his or her apartment because of a civil-authority closure (e.g., there is an evacuation due to a loss at a neighboring property). We are aware that there were at least some ALE claims in New York City as a result of Hurricane Sandy, but we are not sure about the total number of *renters'* ALE claims due to Hurricane Sandy.

Premiums

The price of renter's insurance varies depending on the New York City neighborhood, the amount of personal property coverage purchased (for such items as furniture, jewelry, and electronics), and the liability limit. According to the New York State Department of Financial Services, a basic renter's insurance policy costs around $300 per year for approximately $50,000 worth of property protection. The department's insurance division reported a similar price range for renter's insurance policies in New York State. The insurance division reported that average prices range between $15 and $30 per month (at about $180 to $360 per year).[6]

Take-Up of Renter's Insurance

According to a recent survey by InsuranceQuotes.com, only 34 percent of Americans who rent their homes or apartments have renter's insurance.[7] A 2011 survey from Allstate found a similarly low uptake, with results indicating that only 45 percent of Americans who rent their homes have renter's insurance policies.[8] Surveys indicate that the renter's insurance uptake numbers are low because Americans perceive the price to be much higher than it is. The InsuranceQuotes.com survey found that 60 percent of Americans incorrectly thought that renter's insurance was $250 or more per year. Additionally, 21 percent thought that annual renter's insurance premiums were $1,000 or more.[9] However, according to the National Association of Insurance Commissioners, the average price for renter's insurance is about $185 per year.[10]

---

[5]   New York State Department of Financial Services, undated.

[6]   New York State Department of Financial Services, undated.

[7]   PR Newswire Association, "Almost 2 in 3 Renters Lack Renter's Insurance," San Francisco, Calif., March 11, 2013.

[8]   Allstate, "Survey Finds Less Than Half of Renters Have Renters Insurance," Northbrook, Ill., press release, July 11, 2012.

[9]   PR Newswire Association, 2013.

[10]   PR Newswire Association, 2013.

Flood Insurance Among Renters

The Allstate survey also indicated that 44 percent of Americans believe that they are covered for weather-related floods. However, when survey respondents were asked whether they had a flood insurance policy through the NFIP, only 15 percent of respondents reported having specifically purchased a supplemental flood policy.[11] Thus, according to this survey, about 30 percent of respondents believe that they have flood insurance coverage when they do not.

Condominiums

Condominium coverage includes both a commercial policy for the building owner and a homeowner's policy for the owners of the individual units. Condo building owners buy commercial package policies (CPP) that include property coverage (standard fire, theft, and weather perils), general liability coverage, and workers' compensation coverage for employees. The condo association and the building owner typically work together to shop for coverage and, between the two, ensure that everything is covered. There is not a standard separation between what the building owner carries in coverage and what the association carries.

Individual unit owners purchase homeowner's policies that look similar to renter's policies described above. It covers the walls of the unit, the contents within, ALE, and liability.

Market Share of Insurance Suppliers

Table A.3 lists the top 20 writers of homeowner's insurance in New York City, provided by New York State Insurance Division. These 20 carriers account for about 80 percent of the homeowner's policies in force in New York City. Table A.4 lists the market share of insurers by percentage of Hurricane Sandy claims in New York State.[12]

Coastal Market Assistance Program

C-MAP is for coastal homeowners who have been denied or dropped from insurance coverage.[13] C-MAP was established in 1997 by the New York State Insurance Division and expanded in 2008 with enactment of Section 5414 of the New York State Code

---

[11] Allstate, "Survey Shows a Large Knowledge Gap Amongst Americans When It Comes to Coverage for Flood," Northbrook, Ill., press release, March 21, 2013.

[12] The insurers were asked to report Hurricane Sandy claims statewide; therefore, we do not have the claims specific to New York City.

[13] Information on C-MAP was taken from the C-MAP primer created by Independent Insurance Agents and Brokers of New York (IIABNY) (IIABNY, "Coastal Markets Assistance Program [C-MAP], Agents' and Brokers' Guide to Insuring Coastal Property," May 2009) and New York Property Insurance Underwriting Association (NYPIUA) (NYPIUA, "Coastal Market Assistance Program," undated).

Table A.3
Top 20 Homeowner's Insurance Writers in New York City

Rank	Company
1	State Farm Fire and Casualty Company
2	Allstate Insurance Company
3	Automobile Insurance Company of Hartford, Connecticut
4	Allstate Indemnity Company
5	Castlepoint Insurance Company
6	First Liberty Insurance Corporation
7	Liberty Mutual Fire Insurance Company
8	Tower Insurance Company of New York
9	Metropolitan Property and Casualty Insurance Company
10	Great Northern Insurance Company
11	Pacific Indemnity Company
12	Charter Oak Fire Insurance Company
13	Travco Insurance Company
14	Tri State Consumer Insurance Company
15	Liberty Insurance Corporation
16	Nationwide Mutual Fire Insurance Company
17	Farmington Casualty Company
18	Occidental Fire and Casualty Company of North Carolina
19	Narragansett Bay Insurance Company
20	Chubb Indemnity Insurance Company

for Insurance. Under the expansion, NYPIUA was charged with creating and administering a voluntary program in which insurers, insurance agents, and brokers facilitate efficient access to participating private-market insurance companies to cover personal residential property risks located in coastal areas. NYPIUA insures the dwelling, and private insurers cover contents. Insurance companies voluntarily participate in C-MAP by offering to insure property they might otherwise reject because of proximity to the coast.

Below are the eligibility requirements for C-MAP participation:

• Property must be a one- to four-family owner-occupied dwelling, apartment unit, or condominium unit.

Table A.4
Market Share in New York State, by Percentage of Hurricane Sandy Claims

Company Name	Number of Claims	Percentage of Claims	NFIP Claims for New York State
Allstate Insurance Group	82,094	21	12,084
State Farm	56,304	14	0
Travelers Group	42,013	11	13,280
Berkshire Hathaway (GEICO)	34,173	9	0
Liberty Mutual Group	33,090	8	1,977
Metropolitan Group	21,659	6	790
Tower Group	17,032	4	0
Nationwide Group	15,711	4	3,085
Hartford Fire and Casualty Group	14,928	4	2,449
USAA Group	11,666	3	975
Narragansett Bay Insurance Company	11,129	3	0
New York Property Insurance Underwriting Association	10,830	3	0
NFIP Direct Servicing Agent	—	—	8,788
Fidelity National Property and Casualty Insurance Company	—	—	7,672
American Bankers Insurance Company of Florida	—	—	2,727
Selective Insurance Company of America	—	—	1,150
New York Central Mutual Fire Insurance Company	—	—	598
Other	42,932		
Total claims	393,561		

SOURCE: Number of claims is from New York State Hurricane Sandy Disaster Insurance Assistance, *NYS Insurers Disaster Response Report Card*, March 15, 2013. NFIP claims are from the NFIP.

- Property must be located either (1) on Long Island's South Shore or along the shore of Brooklyn, Queens, Staten Island, and Long Island's Forks, within 1 mile of the shore, or (2) on Long Island's North Shore, the Bronx, or Westchester, within 2,500 feet of the shore.
- The current homeowner must either (1) have received a nonrenewal, a cancellation notice, or conditional nonrenewal from his or her existing insurer for a reason other than nonpayment or (2) have an NYPIUA policy for property located in the areas described above.
- For new purchases, the applicant is required to identify the prior owner's insurer.

- The homeowner must provide evidence of flood insurance if the property is located in an A or V zone as indicated on a federal flood insurance map.

Coverage

C-MAP offers two programs. The first and dominant program (about 95 percent of policies) is the direct method or self-certification program in which the homeowner obtains basic building coverage from NYPIUA as one policy and then a wrap-around endorsement through a private insurer to provide coverage for furnishings, liability, theft, and other needs. Together, these two policies act like a typical homeowner's policy. NYPIUA issues basic coverage policies using the standard deductible published by the Insurance Services Office for its dwelling program. The basic coverage protects property against loss caused by fire, lightning, windstorm, hail, riot, riot attending a strike, civil commotion, aircraft, vehicles, and smoke, and vandalism and malicious mischief. The broad-form coverage includes the perils under basic coverage and property damage by burglars (not theft of property); falling objects; weight of ice, snow, or sleet; accidental discharge of steam; sudden cracking of a steam or hot-water system; freezing; and sudden damage from artificial electric currents.

Coverage limits are as follows:

- building: $600,000
- personal property: $250,000
- rental: $50,000.

Coverage for ALE is available, but the amount of coverage is considered part of the personal property limit. Coverage above these limits may be available up to the statutory limit of $1,500,000 for building and personal property after special consideration by NYPIUA's Appeals Committee.

The second program is a rotation program in which NYPIUA merely acts as the broker, accepting the C-MAP application and then transmitting it to participating private insurers to provide quotes. Once an insurer offers to provide coverage, NYPIUA steps out of the way, and the insurer and applicant communicate directly.

NYPIUA has a special windstorm program for properties within 1,500 feet of the Atlantic Ocean, Long Island Sound, or the Great South Bay or other contiguous bodies of water, regardless of name. This program requires a policyholder to submit an inspection report completed by a licensed architect or engineer who will evaluate the property using special guidelines developed by NYPIUA. Failure to submit the inspection report or failure to comply with recommendations results in the elimination of windstorm coverage.

Deductibles

Deductibles available for dwelling or personal property coverage are $100, $250 (standard), $500, $1,000, or $2,500. Policies with broad-form coverage are subject to a 2-percent windstorm catastrophe deductible for insured properties located in the following counties: Bronx, Kings (Brooklyn), Nassau, Queens, Richmond (Staten Island), Suffolk, and Westchester. This deductible takes effect for windstorm losses 12 hours before and after a hurricane category 2, 3, 4, or 5, as declared by the NWS, makes landfall anywhere in New York State.

Loss Evaluation

The policies are written on an actual-cash-value basis rather than replacement cost (which is the basis for a typical homeowner's policy). Actual cash value is equal to the replacement cost minus any depreciation. However, policies for coastal properties written in conjunction with a voluntary market policy that includes an approved "wrap-around" endorsement can have replacement cost. Upon request of the producer, NYPIUA will provide building coverage on a repair or replacement-cost basis.

National Flood Insurance Program

Background on the National Flood Insurance Program

Flooding is a major source of loss to individuals and businesses in the United States. Private insurers have historically been unable to provide flood insurance at affordable rates in the marketplace; until the establishment of the NFIP in 1968, the primary recourse for flood victims was government disaster assistance.[14] Congress adopted the program in response to the ongoing unavailability of private insurance and continued increases in federal disaster assistance. FEMA, which is part of the U.S. Department of Homeland Security, administers the NFIP.

The NFIP makes flood insurance available to homeowners, renters, and businesses in communities that participate in the NFIP. Such communities agree to adopt and enforce a floodplain management program aimed at reducing their flood losses. The central requirement of the flood management program is that new residential construction in special flood hazard areas (SFHAs) be elevated at or above the level water would reach in a flood that occurs with 1-percent annual chance (the BFE).[15] Existing residential structures that are not built at or above BFE must also be raised to BFE if

---

[14] The catastrophic nature of flooding and private insurers' inability "to develop an actuarial rate structure that could adequately reflect the risk to which flood-prone properties were exposed" are given as the main reasons that the private sector could not provide insurance at a price that a substantial number of people were willing to pay (FEMA, "National Flood Insurance Program: Program Description," August 1, 2002, p. 1).

[15] SFHAs are areas identified on a FEMA FIRM that have at least a 1-percent chance of flooding in any given year. We often refer to these as *high-risk areas* throughout this report. The SFHA does not necessary cover all

they are more than 50 percent damaged by flood. New nonresidential construction in an SFHA must either be elevated or flood-proofed against the 1-percent annual-chance flood.[16]

Early in the program, the federal government found that making insurance available, even at subsidized rates for *existing* buildings, was not a sufficient incentive for communities to join the NFIP or for individuals to purchase flood insurance. In the early 1970s, only 95,000 flood insurance policies were in force, and only a few thousand communities participated in the program.[17] In response, Congress passed the Flood Disaster Protection Act of 1973,[18] which obligates federally regulated lenders to require flood insurance as a condition of granting or continuing a loan when the buildings and improvements securing it are in the SFHA of a community participating in the NFIP. Loans on homes in SFHAs sold to government-sponsored enterprises, such as Fannie Mae and Freddie Mac, are also subject to this MPR. The act prohibits federal agencies from providing financial assistance for acquisition or construction of buildings and certain disaster assistance in the SFHA of any community that did not join in the NFIP by July 1, 1975, or within one year of being identified as flood-prone.[19] The MPR was strengthened by the National Flood Insurance Reform Act of 1994.[20] The number of communities participating in the program and the number of policyholders grew dramatically as a result. Currently, more than 20,000 communities participate in the program and more than 5.6 million flood policies are in place. To make the program more self-supporting, FEMA started to reduce subsidies in the 1980s.[21]

In times when claims are higher than average, the NFIP has the ability to borrow from the U.S. Treasury—a loan that would have to be repaid with interest. The NFIP experienced significant financial difficulty beginning in 2005 with multiple high-cost storms, including Katrina and Rita. Its borrowing increased, and its repayments lapsed, resulting in an $18 billion deficit by 2012. To correct this imbalance, Congress required structural changes to the program in a new law that passed (BW-12). The legislation is designed to make the NFIP financially stronger by eliminating the artificially low rates and making them more actuarially sound to reflect the full risk. Two

---

the flood-prone areas in a community. Small, noncontiguous areas in an NFIP community that have at least a 1-percent chance of flooding, for example, are often not identified on a FIRM.

[16] FEMA, 2002, p. 13.

[17] FEMA, 2002, p. 3.

[18] Public Law 93-134, Flood Disaster Protection Act of 1973, October 19, 1973.

[19] FEMA, 2002, p. 3.

[20] Public Law 103-325, Riegle Community Development and Regulatory Improvement Act of 1994, September 23, 1994, Title V.

[21] Warren Kriesel and Craig Landry, "Participation in the National Flood Insurance Program: An Empirical Analysis for Coastal Properties," *Journal of Risk and Insurance*, Vol. 71, No. 3, September 2004, pp. 405–420, p. 417.

specific areas are being affected: the elimination of subsidized pre-FIRM rates and the elimination of the grandfathering rating. Pre-FIRM buildings are ones that were built before the first FIRM became effective for a specific community. FEMA estimates that the rates for pre-FIRM structures represent about 45 percent of the true actuarial rates. Consequently, they are referred to as *subsidized rates*. The grandfathering of rates allows properties that are being mapped into a higher-risk zone to continue to use their current lower-risk zone for future rating when the new FIRM becomes effective. Taken together, this can mean significant rate increases for property owners in coastal areas. Chapter Four discusses the changes resulting from BW-12 in more detail.

National Flood Insurance Premium Coverage Types

For residential buildings and individual condominium units, the NFIP offers a maximum $250,000 in structure coverage and up to $100,000 in contents coverage.[22] Deductibles apply separately to buildings and contents. The standard residential deductible is $1,000, but higher deductibles are available. Nonresidential buildings are eligible for up to $500,000 in structure coverage and $500,000 in contents coverage.[23] Commercial deductibles are available up to $50,000. Flood insurance in excess of these NFIP limits is available from the private market.

For structure coverage, the NFIP pays up to the replacement cost (residential) or actual cash value (commercial) of the actual damages or the policy limit of liability, whichever is less. The NFIP pays actual cash value on contents coverage. The NFIP provides limited coverage for damage below the lowest elevated floor, such as basements. For example, mechanical equipment in the basement, such as a furnace or central air system, is covered, but finished drywall is not. *Basement* is defined as any area of the building having its floor below ground level on all sides. This would include a sunken room or a sunken portion of a room. The NFIP does not cover additional living expenses for temporary housing.

Coverage for mixed-use buildings under the NFIP is not very precise. If the building contains more than 25 percent commercial space, the policy is considered nonresidential, and the $500,000 structure and $500,000 contents limits apply. But if a business is at the bottom of a residential building (total building is less than 25 percent commercial), it is limited to the residential policy limits of $250,000 for structure, though it can buy a $500,000 limit for contents. Only 10 percent of that $500,000 contents policy can be used to cover repairs to the structure.

---

[22] Residential condominium buildings can purchase up to $250,000 multiplied by the number of units and up to $100,000 in commonly owned contents coverage per building (FEMA, 2002, p. 25).

[23] FEMA, 2002, p. 25.

Condominium Coverage

The Residential Condominium Building Association Policy (RCBAP) provides coverage for condominiums for which at least 75 percent of the building's floor is for residential use. This includes garden apartment–type construction, townhouses, row houses, and single-family detached buildings operated by condominium associations. The limit of coverage is the lesser of 100 percent of the replacement-cost value of the building or the total number of units times $250,000. The policy provides coverage for the building and common areas and commonly owned contents. Replacement-cost coverage is available for the building if the limit is at least 80 percent of the condominium's replacement cost (or the maximum limits allowed, whichever is smaller); otherwise, a co-insurance penalty will be applied at the time of loss. The RCBAP does not cover the contents of the individual units. Contents coverage, which must be purchased separately by individual unit owners, is available up to $100,000 and based on actual cash value.

A unit owner may buy insurance to cover his or her personal property within that unit using the dwelling policy form. If a unit owner's lender does not feel that the unit is adequately covered by the association's RCBAP, additional building coverage can be purchased by the unit owner under the dwelling policy form. The total of a unit owner's building coverage plus his or her share of RCBAP building coverage may not exceed $250,000.

Purchase Requirements

Property Insurance

Most mortgage lenders require that homeowners and businesses carry property and casualty insurance, though this is not a federal government requirement like the MPR for flood insurance, as is discussed below.

Flood Insurance

As referenced earlier, the 1994 National Flood Insurance Reform Act initiated the MPR. Under this provision, any building (residential or commercial) secured by a loan from a federally regulated lender must carry flood insurance if it lies in an SFHA. This applies for the duration of the loan or any time during the term of the loan when the building is inside the SFHA. During our interviews with representatives from the insurance industry, it was generally thought that compliance with the MPR was quite low prior to Hurricane Sandy. Those we interviewed noted that compliance is likely to go up significantly because of the fines for noncompliance imposed on lending institutions under BW-12. BW-12 raised the fines from $350 to $2,000 for each property out of compliance. Some of those we interviewed speculated that $350 was not steep enough to induce greater compliance among lenders but that increasing the fine more than sixfold should have an effect. Several interviewees noted that compliance would go up only if enforcement also increases.

In our interviews, we also heard that most of the non–federally regulated lenders also require insurance and flood insurance, depending on the building's location, to secure their investment, though compliance is not enforced by the federal government like it is under the MPR.

National Flood Insurance Program Premiums

Flood insurance premiums are calculated using several factors, including flood zone, elevation, and date of construction relative to the date of the community's first FIRM and some characteristics of the house if it is in a high-risk flood area. FEMA reports that the average flood insurance policy is about $625 per year.[24] FEMA definitions of the various flood zones can be found in Table A.5. The high-risk flood zones begin with A or V.

Table A.6 provides example premiums for a set limit of coverage ($200,000 in building and $80,000 in contents) for a single-family primary residence. The examples vary by flood zone, elevation, and pre- and post-FIRM construction. These rates apply nationwide and do not refer specifically to New York City. Note that post-FIRM prices are often below pre-FIRM subsidized rates. The post-FIRM buildings were built to different standards and benefit from the reduced risk of flooding due to those standards.

National Flood Insurance Program Coverage Limitations in Areas Below the Lowest Elevated Floor and Basements

There are three policy forms used by the NFIP:

- dwelling form: This form is issued to homeowners, residential renters, and condominium unit owners or owners of residential buildings containing two to four units.
- general property form: This form is issued to owners of residential buildings with five or more units, owners or lessees of nonresidential buildings or units, and owners or lessees of nonresidential buildings or units.
- RCBAP form: This form is issued to residential condominium associations on behalf of association and unit owners.

Basement is defined in each policy form as any area of the building, including any sunken room or sunken portion of a room, having its floor below ground level (subgrade) on all sides. Flood insurance coverage for basements is limited to more-mechanical items and does not coverage such items as furnishings regardless of zone or date of construction.

Each policy form provides the same coverage limitations in basements. Under coverage A (building property), the following items in a basement are covered, if

---

[24] NFIP, "NFIP Statistics," last updated September 26, 2013a.

Table A.5
Federal Emergency Management Agency Flood-Zone Designations

Zone	Description
A	Area with a 1% annual chance of flooding and a 26% chance of flooding over the life of a 30-year mortgage
AE, A1–A30	The base floodplain where BFEs are provided
AH	Area with a 1% annual chance of shallow flooding, usually in the form of a pond, with an average depth ranging from 1 to 3 feet. These areas have a 26% chance of flooding over the life of a 30-year mortgage. BFEs derived from detailed analyses are shown on the flood map at selected intervals within these zones.
AO	River or stream flood hazard area or area with a 1% or greater chance of shallow flooding each year, usually in the form of sheet flow, with an average depth ranging from 1 to 3 feet. These areas have a 26% chance of flooding over the life of a 30-year mortgage. Average flood depths derived from detailed analyses are shown on the flood map within these zones.
AR	Area with a temporarily increased flood risk due to the building or restoration of a flood-control system (such as a levee or a dam). MPRs for flood insurance will apply, but rates will not exceed the rates for unnumbered A zones if the structure is built or restored in compliance with Zone AR floodplain management regulations.
AR99	Area with a 1% annual chance of flooding that will be protected by a federal flood-control system in which construction has reached specified legal requirements. No depths or BFEs are shown on the flood map within these zones.
V	Coastal area with a 1% or greater chance of flooding and an additional hazard associated with storm waves. These areas have a 26% chance of flooding over the life of a 30-year mortgage. No BFEs are shown on the flood map within these zones.
VE, V1–V30	Coastal area with a 1% or greater chance of flooding and an additional hazard associated with storm waves. These areas have a 26% chance of flooding over the life of a 30-year mortgage. BFEs derived from detailed analyses are shown on the flood map at selected intervals within these zones.
B and X (shaded area of map)	Area of moderate flood hazard, usually the area between the limits of the 100-year and 500-year floods. Also used to designate base floodplains of lesser hazards, such as areas protected by levees from 100-year flood, or shallow flooding areas with average depths of less than 1 foot or drainage areas less than 1 square mile.
C and X (unshaded area of map)	Area of minimal flood hazard, usually depicted on FIRM as above the 500-year flood level
D	Area with possible but undetermined flood hazards. No flood hazard analysis has been conducted. Flood insurance rates are commensurate with the uncertainty of the flood risk.

SOURCE: Map Service Center, Federal Emergency Management Agency, "Definitions of FEMA Flood Zone Designations," undated; referenced April 23, 2013.

installed in their functioning locations and, if necessary for operation, connected to a power source:

- central air conditioners
- cisterns and the water in them

Table A.6
National Flood Insurance Program Premium Comparisons for a Policy with $200,000 in Building Coverage and $80,000 in Contents Coverage

Pre- or Post-FIRM[a]	Dwelling Type	Deductible Building/Contents ($)	Flood Zone	Elevation Difference of Lowest Floor and BFE (feet)	Annual Flood Insurance Premium ($)[b]
Either pre or post	Single Family One floor No basement	1,000/1,000	B, C, or X	Not needed	388[c]
Pre	Primary Single family One floor No basement[d]	2,000/2,000	A1–30, AE, AO, AH, A	Not needed	2,643
Post	Single family One floor No basement	1,000/1,000	Unnumbered A zone (no estimated BFE)	5 2 to 4 1	597 1,236 2,763
Post	Single family One floor No basement	1,000/1,000	A1–30, AE	4 2 0 −1	462 570 1,636 5,042
Pre	Primary single family without enclosure	2,000/2,000	V1–V30, VE	Not needed	5,554
Pre	Primary single family with enclosure	2,000/2,000	V1–V30, VE	Not needed	7,648
Post	Single family without obstruction	1,000/1,000	V1–V30, VE	4 or more 2 0 −1	2,090 3,254 6,898 9,282
Post	Single family with obstruction	1,000/1,000	V1–V30, VE	4 or more 2 0 −1	4,110 5,414 8,130 10,486

[a] Pre-FIRM = construction on or before December 31, 1974, or before the effective date of the initial FIRM for the community, whichever is later. For New York City, the first flood map was created in 1983 so any buildings constructed before that year are considered pre-FIRM.

[b] Premiums are as of January 1, 2013; premiums include the federal policy fee and increased cost-of-compliance fee. Premiums in this table were calculated using the NFIP rate tables.

[c] For a PRP. Preferred-risk eligibility: Starting January 1, 2011, the eligibility period for PRPs was extended.

[d] For flood insurance rating purposes, a primary residence is a building that will be lived in by the insured or the insured's spouse for at least 80 percent of the 365 days following the policy effective date. If the building will be lived in for less than 80 percent of the policy year, it is considered to be a nonprimary residence. Secondary residences' rates are set 25 percent higher starting January 1, 2013.

- drywall for walls and ceilings in a basement and the cost of labor to nail it, unfinished, unfloated, and not taped, to the framing
- electrical-junction and circuit-breaker boxes
- electrical outlets and switches
- elevators, dumbwaiters, and related equipment, except for related equipment installed below the BFE after September 30, 1987
- fuel tanks and the fuel in them
- furnaces and hot-water heaters
- heat pumps
- nonflammable insulation in a basement
- pumps and tanks used in solar energy systems
- stairways and staircases attached to the building, not separated from it by elevated walkways
- sump pumps
- water softeners and the chemicals in them, water filters, and faucets installed as an integral part of the plumbing system
- well-water tanks and pumps
- required utility connections for any item in this list
- footings, foundations, posts, pilings, piers, or other foundation walls and anchorage systems required to support a building.

Under coverage B (personal property), the following items are *not* insured by either building property or personal property coverage:

- paneling, bookcases, shelving, or window treatments, such as curtains or blinds
- carpeting, area carpets, or other floor coverings, such as tile
- drywall for walls or ceilings (below the lowest elevated floor and not in a basement)
- walls or ceilings not made of drywall
- most personal property, such as clothing, electronic equipment, kitchen supplies, or furniture
- refrigerators or the food in them.

The following items *are* covered in basements, if installed in their functioning locations and, if necessary for operation, connected to a power source:

- air-conditioning units, portable or window type
- clothes washers and dryers
- food freezers, other than walk-in
- food in any freezer.

With a PRP, contents located entirely in a basement are not eligible for contents-only coverage.

Elevating electrical and other related equipment outside the basement will reduce the premium in specific situations. If the basement floor is at least 2 feet below the BFE, moving the machinery and equipment at or above the BFE will qualify for a reduced rate. These are submit-for-rate (an agent cannot rate the risk and must submit it to their insurance company to rate or FEMA to rate), and they are not published in the flood insurance manual. In multifamily and nonresidential buildings, moving contents to the second floor will produce a lower rate. This rating option does not apply to single-family residences because it is assumed that contents are throughout the house.

Commercial Insurance

Commercial insurance differs depending on the size of the firm needing coverage but typically includes property and casualty coverage[25] and sometimes business-interruption insurance. According to the interviews we conducted with insurance industry experts, the general size categories for commercial firms are large, middle-market, or small. The level of comprehensive insurance coverage can vary widely from one category to the other, especially as it relates to flood insurance and business-interruption insurance. Business-interruption insurance covers loss of business income due to interruption of operations caused by a direct physical loss at the premises. Additional endorsements can be purchased to cover utility interruptions, such as power outages. According to our discussions with insurance brokers and agents who service various sizes of commercial business, as well as other insurance industry officials, the percentage of firms that purchase some type of property and casualty coverage across all sizes of firms is thought to be quite high (80–90 percent). Insurance for flood damage or business interruption declines significantly as the firm size decreases. There is no standard method within the insurance industry of defining firm size. Some carriers and brokers define firm size by the amount of premium paid per year, while others define size based on complexity of the account or whether the firm has a risk manager. In our interviews, several carriers and brokers referred to firm size by the amount of premium paid per year, and that is how we define the market categories in this section.

Large Firms

Large firms are those that pay more than $500,000 in premiums per year. Large businesses tend to bundle together property loss, business interruption, supply chain, liability, flood, and other perils into a single policy called a *manuscript property policy*. According to our insurance industry interviews, there is thought to be very high

---

[25] Casualty includes liability coverage.

uptake of flood insurance among these firms. Large firms tend to have these policies regardless of whether they are in or out of the high-risk flood zones. The manuscript policies include a standard flood insurance policy, but the limits and coverage types can vary by policyholder. It is thought that a small percentage (some brokers estimated less than 25 percent) of these large businesses in the city buy NFIP coverage specifically to cover part of their deductible. The standard flood deductible in the private insurance market for commercial buildings is 3–5 percent of the value of the insured property. According to those we interviewed, it is not uncommon for large firms to self-insure for the first $1 million of flood coverage and to buy flood coverage for anything over that amount.

The brokers we interviewed described how securing flood insurance coverage for their clients has changed over the years. In years past, brokers were able to piece together coverage behind the manuscript policy from two to three insurers. Now they often have to layer coverage from many different companies to fully cover their clients' flood insurance needs. For example, they will find one firm that is willing to cover flood damages up to the first $5 million, a second firm to cover $5 million to $25 million, a third firm to cover $25 million to $50 million, and so on. Reinsurers have been pushing insurance companies to lower their exposure to flood coverage. As a result, brokers more frequently need to secure four or five separate insurers to provide full coverage for a client. The brokers reported that they are not experiencing difficulty in finding private flood insurance providers; they just have to find more of them for each client.

Middle-Market Firms

This is the largest category of the market in terms of number of firms and encompasses firms whose insurance premiums range from more than $50,000 to less than $500,000 per year. There are three main tranches of middle-market firms. The larger ones at the higher end of the premium spectrum will buy manuscript policies similar to the larger firms that include the standard flood coverage, but the number of firms that fall into this category is thought to be quite small. These firms may buy NFIP policies to reduce their deductibles.

The largest middle tranche does not purchase a manuscript policy but instead pieces together various policies to meet its needs, an approach that sometimes referred to as a *package policy*. This includes using the NFIP for flood coverage, if the business decides to purchase flood insurance. Some in this tranche will buy excess coverage in the private market on top of the NFIP coverage, and the excess typically includes business-interruption insurance related to the flooding event (the standard business-interruption coverage would exclude flood damage).

The smaller firms in this middle market (between $50,000 and $200,000 in premiums per year) may not carry any flood insurance, and those that do purchase it primarily through the NFIP and go bare over the $500,000 policy limits.[26]

Middle-market firms are not likely to have business-interruption coverage for flooding unless they have manuscript or package policies or have purchased excess flood policies.

Small Firms

The small firms tend to buy a business owner's policy, which is similar to a standard homeowner's policy with a few differences. The big difference is higher contents and liability limits (contents limits can often exceed building structure limits for firms with expensive equipment) and the inclusion of business-interruption coverage. According to those we interviewed, very few small firms carry flood insurance, and many do not carry business-interruption insurance.

The Private Flood Insurance Market

There are two general types of providers of flood insurance: those in the admitted market, often referred to as the *voluntary* or *standard line insurers*, and those in the nonadmitted market, also referred to as *surplus line insurers*. All providers of insurance are licensed in the state regardless of whether they are admitted or nonadmitted. Both admitted and nonadmitted insurers can provide insurance coverage to both homeowners and commercial firms. Some insurers have subsidiaries that operate in the admitted market and subsidiaries that operate in the surplus market.

Admitted carriers submit their applications, policy forms, endorsements, and rating structure for approval by the New York State Department of Financial Services. One of the benefits for consumers of purchasing insurance in the admitted market is that the state has the responsibility to pay an insurer's claims in the event of insolvency.

Surplus line insurers provide coverage for risks not typically covered in the traditional insurance marketplace. Surplus line insurers will frequently provide coverage in excess of a primary policy from an admitted carrier but can also provide first-dollar coverage. Most of these policies are purchased by commercial firms to cover commercial risks. These insurers have much more pricing flexibility because they do not submit their rates for review by the state. Because these are business-to-business transactions, the surplus line market is less regulated than insurance in the admitted market, and the policies are not protected by guaranty funds from the state in the event of insolvency.

The Excess Flood Market

Residential and commercial property owners that are looking for policy limits that exceed those allowed under the NFIP will often seek additional flood coverage in

---

[26] *Go bare* means that the policyholder does not have insurance coverage for losses over $500,000.

what is called the excess market primarily provided by surplus line carriers. According to those we interviewed, Lloyd's of London is probably the leading provider of excess flood coverage above NFIP policy limits. Its carriers are made up of property syndicates. The lead syndicate may put up the first 25 percent of coverage, and then other syndicates will come in and put up additional layers until it reaches 100 percent of the needed coverage. According to those we interviewed, there are typically six to eight syndicates that contribute to the 100 percent needed for each property owner. In total, there are about 12 syndicates at Lloyd's that participate in providing flood coverage, and they take turns being the lead syndicate. Some of the excess programs start providing coverage only at the NFIP policy limits ($250,000 for residential and $500,000 for commercial), while others will offer first-dollar flood coverage but not for properties in the A and V zones.

Some of these programs have the same exclusions as the NFIP, such as limited basement coverage, while others will cover more items in basements. Some programs provide actual cash value rather than replacement-cost coverage, but they will have an endorsement for replacement value that can be purchased at an additional cost. These programs do typically cover business-interruption expenses, and some will offer ALE on the residential side.

Private Flood Insurance Providers

Both admitted carriers and surplus line carriers provide private flood insurance to both homeowners and commercial firms. Some of the residential providers in New York include such carriers as Chubb, AIG, Fireman's Fund, Lexington, and Chartis. They all offer flood coverage that includes ALE and basement coverage, and we are told they are a bit more expensive than the NFIP. These firms carry most of the exposure themselves (rather than layering the coverage with different insurers), though they may lay off some exposure to reinsurers.

Insurers that provide commercial coverage include most of the same carriers that provide private residential flood insurance. Other carriers, such as Affiliated FM, Hartford, Zurich, and Travelers, provide all risk programs that include flood. Some of these carriers offer first-dollar coverage, and others start offering coverage only at $500,000. It is up to the firm purchasing the coverage whether it wants to use the NFIP for that first layer of coverage or if it wants to self-insure.

Differences in National Flood Insurance Program and Private Flood Coverage

The NFIP will write in almost all locations, with the exception of areas identified by the Coastal Barrier Resources Act (CBRA) or in nonparticipating communities.[27] A

---

[27] Public Law 97-348, Coastal Barrier Resources Act, October 18, 1982. The CBRA removed the federal government from financial involvement associated with building and development in undeveloped portions of designated coastal barriers. CBRA banned the sale of NFIP flood insurance for structures built or substantially improved on or after a specified date.

property in an A or V zone has no difficulty getting coverage with the NFIP within its policy limits even if there have been repetitive losses. The private markets are much more selective about properties they will write in A and V zones. According to the insurance industry representatives we interviewed, once a location has experienced a loss, private insurers are not likely to provide any flood coverage for that location.

Property owners (residential and commercial) seeking higher policy limits or seeking basement coverage and ALE or business-interruption coverage will turn to the private markets. Owners of a single commercial building or just a few commercial buildings are the ones who tend to buy NFIP coverage. If a business wants coverage on multiple buildings, the package policies offered in the private market allow much more flexibility. Those policies will allow all the buildings to be covered under one policy (whereas the NFIP requires one policy per structure) and are flexible in terms of deductibles and higher policy limits. These policies will often include coverage for basements and business interruption. Often, access to the business-interruption and extra-expense coverage types resulting from a flood is as important as the actual flood coverage.

Because the private market can be selective in the properties it carries, its risk appetite could change at any time, resulting in loss of coverage to a property and the disruption this entails. This uncertainty would not be present under the NFIP.

National Flood Insurance Program Take-Up Rates in the High-Risk Areas of the Preliminary Work Map

Tables B.1 and B.2 provide estimates of the number and take-up rates in the high-risk zones of the PWM. (In contrast, Tables 4.3 and 4.4 in Chapter Four show take-up in the high-risk areas added by the PWM.) High-risk areas subject to riverine flooding are not included in the results that follow, but inclusion of the riverine areas is not

Table B.1
Take-Up Rates for National Flood Insurance Program Policies in the High-Risk Zones of the Preliminary Work Map on One- to Four-Family Structures (as of October 31, 2012)

Measure	Estimate
Take-up rate (percentage of structures with NFIP policy) (based on 38,806 parcels)[a]	28
Lower bound for take-up rate (based on 43,661 parcels)	28
Upper bound for take-up rate (based on 43,661 parcels)	34

SOURCE: Merge of NFIP policy file with New York City parcel data.

[a] Based on parcels with one structure.

Table B.2
Take-Up Rates for One- to Four-Family Structures with Mortgages in the High-Risk Zones of the Preliminary Work Map (as of October 31, 2012)

Structure	Percentage Estimate
Structures with mortgages (based on 34,018 parcels)	78
Take-up rate for structures with mortgages (based on 26,695 parcels)	35
Take-up rate for structures without mortgages (based on 7,323 parcels)	16

NOTE: Based on parcels with one structure.

expected to change the results much. The riverine areas amounted to about 8 percent of the high-risk areas in the 2007 FIRM. Because the high-risk area of the PWM is larger and the riverine areas are not being revised, the percentage will be lower for the PWM.

Development of Scenarios of Premium Change Analysis

This appendix describes the process for selecting the structure elevation scenarios used in the cases that illustrate NFIP premium changes due to the new flood map in New York City (Tables 4.8 and 4.10 in Chapter Four). The process for pre-FIRM structures is described first, followed by that for post-FIRM structures.

Pre-FIRM Structures

To create a range of plausible scenarios for one- to four-family pre-FIRM structures, we proceeded in two steps: We developed first a range for the difference between structure elevation and ground level (also referred to as *grade*) and second a range for the difference between ground level and water height in a 100-year flood (BFE).

City staff with whom we spoke explained that there are two main types of basements in the city. One is referred to as a *cellar* and is typically mostly below grade. The other is referred to as a *basement* and is typically only partly below grade. Basements might be used, for example, as garden apartments. According to city staff, cellar floors are typically 8 feet below grade, and basement floors are typically 4 feet below grade. We thus set structure elevation relative to grade at −4 and −8 in the scenarios for buildings with basements or cellars. For buildings without basements or cellars, we set the structure elevations to 1 foot above grade.

The range chosen for the difference between BFE and ground level is based on analysis conducted by New York City's OLTPS. For each parcel in the high-risk zone of the PWM, OLTPS calculated the average difference between BFE and ground level. Using the results shown in Table C.1, we selected a range of 1 to 5 feet.

Table C.2 combines structure elevation relative to grade and BFE relative to grade to generate a range of scenarios for the difference between BFE and structure elevation. As can be seen in the table, elevations from −5 to −13 are plausible for pre-FIRM structures with basements or cellars. For buildings without basements or cellars, elevations between 0 and −4 would not be unusual. Structures with elevations outside these intervals would also undoubtedly be observed.

Table C.1
Distance from Base Flood Elevation to Ground Level in High-Risk Areas of the Preliminary Work Map, 61,668 Parcels

Average Distance in Parcel from BFE to Ground Level (feet)	Percentage of Parcels
<0	4
≥0 and <1	19
≥1 and <2	20
≥2 and <3	18
≥3 and <4	14
≥4 and <5	10
≥5 and <6	5
≥6 and <7	3
≥7 and <8	2
≥8 and <9	2
≥9 and <10	1
≥10	2
Total	100

SOURCE: OLTPS data provided in September 2013.

Table C.2
Selection of Elevation Differences for Pre-FIRM Scenarios

Scenario	Type of Basement	Structure Elevation Relative to Grade	BFE Relative to Grade in PWM	Structure Relative to BFE in PWM
A	Basement	−4	1	−5
B	Cellar	−8	1	−9
C	Basement	−4	5	−9
D	Cellar	−8	5	−13
E	None	1	1	0
F	None	1	5	−4

Post-FIRM Structures

To develop scenarios for the pricing examples for post-FIRM properties, we start with data on the difference between structure elevation and the BFE according to the 2007 FIRM. Elevation data are available in the NFIP policy file for insured post-FIRM structures in high-risk areas. We chose −5 to 3 feet as a reasonable range for the elevation of post-FIRM structures with basements relative to the 2007 BFE.[1] These values roughly correspond to the 10th and 90th percentiles of the elevation differences for post-FIRM one- to four-family structures with basements in the high-risk zone of the 2007 FIRM. As discussed in Chapter Four, further investigation of the reliability of the basement data is needed before conclusions can be made about the frequency of basements in post-FIRM structures in the high-risk areas. For structures without basements, we similarly selected −1 to 4 feet. As shown in Table C.3, these elevations are then combined with a reasonable range for the change of the BFE in the PWM to produce a range of structure elevations relative to the BFE indicated by the PWM.

Table C.3
Development of Pricing Scenarios for Post-FIRM One- to Four-Family Structures

Scenario	Basement	Structure Elevation Relative to BFE Indicated by 2007 FIRM	Change in BFE	Structure Elevation Relative to BFE Indicated by PWM
A	Yes	3	2	1
B	Yes	−5	2	−7
C	Yes	3	4	−1
D	Yes	−5	4	−9
E	No	4	2	2
F	No	−1	2	−3
G	No	4	4	0
H	No	−1	4	−5

---

[1] We now use the term *basement* to refer to both basements and cellars, as used by New York City.

Bibliography

Advisen, "The State of the Commercial Property/Casualty Insurance Market," January 2013. As of April 23, 2013:
http://corner.advisen.com/pdf_files/2012_Zurich_SOM2_Paper.pdf

Allstate, "Survey Finds Less Than Half of Renters Have Renters Insurance," Northbrook, Ill., press release, July 11, 2012. As of April 23, 2013:
http://www.allstatenewsroom.com/channels/News-Releases/releases/
survey-finds-less-than-half-of-renters-have-renters-insurance

———, "Survey Shows a Large Knowledge Gap Amongst Americans When It Comes to Coverage for Flood," Northbrook, Ill., press release, March 21, 2013. As of April 23, 2013:
http://www.allstatenewsroom.com/channels/News-Releases/releases/
survey-shows-a-large-knowledge-gap-amongst-americans-when-it-comes-to-coverage-for-flood-1

Bin, Okmyung, Jamie Brown Kruse, and Craig E. Landry, "Flood Hazards, Insurance Rates, and Amenities: Evidence from the Coastal Housing Market," *Journal of Risk and Insurance*, Vol. 75, No. 1, March 2008, pp. 63–82.

Camerer, Colin F., and Howard Kunreuther, "Decision Processes for Low Probability Events: Policy Implications," *Journal of Policy Analysis and Management*, Vol. 8, No. 4, 1989, pp. 565–592.

Caruso, David B., "New York to Compensate Storm Victims for NFIP's 'Earth Movement' Exclusion," *Insurance Journal*, September 30, 2013. As of October 16, 2013:
http://www.insurancejournal.com/news/east/2013/09/30/306636.htm

Choi, James J., David Laibson, Brigitte C. Madrian, and Andrew Metrick, *Saving for Retirement on the Path of Least Resistance*, Philadelphia, Pa.: Rodney L. White Center for Financial Research, Wharton School, University of Pennsylvania, September 2005. As of April 23, 2013:
http://finance.wharton.upenn.edu/~rlwctr/papers/0509.pdf

CIAB—*See* Council of Insurance Agents and Brokers.

City of New York, "A Stronger, More Resilient New York," June 2013. As of June 2013:
http://www.nyc.gov/html/sirr/html/report/report.shtml

Council of Insurance Agents and Brokers, "Commercial P/C Pricing Took Leap in Second Quarter, According to Council Survey," news release, July 31, 2012a.

———, "Commercial P/C Pricing Slowed in Third Quarter, According to the Council's Survey," news release, November 1, 2012b.

———, "Commercial P/C Pricing Rose 4th Quarter; Underwriting Remained Tight, According to the Council's Survey," news release, February 5, 2013a.

————, "Commercial P/C Pricing Continued Upward Trend in First Quarter, According to the Council's Survey," news release, April 18, 2013b.

————, "Commercial P/C Pricing Increases Slowed in Second Quarter, According to CIAB Survey," news release, July 23, 2013c.

Dixon, Lloyd, Noreen Clancy, Bruce Bender, and Patricia K. Ehrler, *The Lender-Placed Flood Insurance Market for Residential Properties*, Santa Monica, Calif.: RAND Corporation, TR-468-FEMA, 2007. As of October 11, 2013:
http://www.rand.org/pubs/technical_reports/TR468.html

Dixon, Lloyd, Noreen Clancy, Seth A. Seabury, and Adrian Overton, *The National Flood Insurance Program's Market Penetration Rate: Estimates and Policy Implications*, Santa Monica, Calif.: RAND Corporation, TR-300-FEMA, 2006. As of October 11, 2013:
http://www.rand.org/pubs/technical_reports/TR300.html

Edwards, A. G. K., G. Naik, H. Ahmed, G. J. Elwyn, T. Pickles, K. Hood, and R. Playle, "Personalised Risk Communication for Informed Decision Making About Taking Screening Tests," *Cochrane Database of Systematic Reviews*, Vol. 2, February 28, 2013.

Federal Emergency Management Agency, "National Flood Insurance Program: Program Description," August 1, 2002. As of October 11, 2013:
http://www.fema.gov/media-library-data/20130726-1447-20490-2156/nfipdescrip_1_.pdf

————, *Flood Map Modernization Mid-Course Adjustment: Executive Overview*, March 27, 2006. As of October 11, 2013:
http://www.fema.gov/media-library-data/20130726-1541-20490-0862/mm_mcaovr.txt

————, "Repetitive Loss," August 15, 2007. As of October 16, 2013:
http://www.fema.gov/media-library/assets/documents/11353

————, "What Is Risk MAP?" October 2012. As of October 11, 2013:
http://www.fema.gov/media-library-data/20130726-1731-25045-5094/what_is_risk_map.pdf

————, "Who Will Be Impacted by Rate Increases Nationally Under Section 205?" April 2013a. As of October 11, 2013:
http://www.fema.gov/media-library-data/20130726-1910-25045-4019/bw12_impact_fs_04092013_natl_508.pdf

————, "Significant Flood Events as of June 30, 2013," c. July 2013b.

————, "Severe Repetitive Loss Program," last updated August 2, 2013c. As of October 16, 2013:
http://www.fema.gov/severe-repetitive-loss-program

————, *Flood Insurance Manual, Effective October 1, 2013*, September 23, 2013d. As of October 21, 2013:
http://www.fema.gov/media-library/assets/documents/34745

————, *National Flood Insurance Program: Specific Rating Guidelines*, October 2013e. As of October 11, 2013:
http://www.fema.gov/media-library-data/e89943abe296767c5579d37c7d24dc90/SRG+October_2013_508.pdf

————, "Community Status Book Report: Nation—Communities Participating in the National Flood Program," October 10, 2013f; referenced April 23, 2013. As of October 11, 2013:
http://www.fema.gov/cis/nation.html

FEMA—*See* Federal Emergency Management Agency.

Furman Center for Real Estate and Urban Policy and Moelis Institute for Affordable Housing Policy, New York University, "Sandy's Effects on Housing in New York City," fact brief, March 2013. As of October 11, 2013:
http://furmancenter.org/files/publications/SandysEffectsOnHousingInNYC.pdf

GAO—*See* U.S. Government Accountability Office.

Harrison, David M., Greg T. Smersh, and Arthur L. Schwartz, Jr., "Environmental Determinants of Housing Prices: The Impact of Flood Zone Status," *Journal of Real Estate Research*, Vol. 21, No. 1–2, 2001, pp. 3–20.

Hartwig, Robert P., "The Insurance Industry's Response to Superstorm Sandy: Putting the Northeast on the Road to Recovery," Washington, D.C.: Insurance Information Institute, press briefing, December 10, 2012. As of April 23, 2013:
http://www.iii.org/presentations/the-insurance-industrys-response-to-superstorm-sandy-putting-the-northeast-on-the-road-recovery-press-briefing.html

Independent Insurance Agents and Brokers of New York, "Coastal Markets Assistance Program (C-MAP), Agents' and Brokers' Guide to Insuring Coastal Property," May 2009.

Kousky, Carolyn, and Howard Kunreuther, "Addressing Affordability in the National Flood Insurance Program," Washington, D.C.: Resources for the Future and the Wharton Risk Management and Decision Processes Center, Issue Brief 13-02, August 2013. As of October 11, 2013:
http://www.rff.org/Publications/Pages/PublicationDetails.aspx?PublicationID=22247

Kriesel, Warren, and Craig Landry, "Participation in the National Flood Insurance Program: An Empirical Analysis for Coastal Properties," *Journal of Risk and Insurance*, Vol. 71, No. 3, September 2004, pp. 405–420.

Kunreuther, Howard, and Erwann O. Michel-Kerjan, "Managing Catastrophes Through Insurance: Challenges and Opportunities for Reducing Future Risks," Philadelphia, Pa.: Wharton Risk Management and Decision Processes Center, Working Paper 2009-11-30, November 2009. As of April 23, 2013:
http://opim.wharton.upenn.edu/risk/library/WP20091130_HK,EMK_ReducingFutureRisks.pdf

Lusardi, Annamaria, and Olivia S. Mitchell, "Financial Literacy and Retirement Preparedness: Evidence and Implications for Financial Education," *Business Economics*, Vol. 42, No. 1, January 2007, pp. 35–44.

Map Service Center, Federal Emergency Management Agency, "Definitions of FEMA Flood Zone Designations," undated; referenced April 23, 2013. As of October 11, 2013:
https://msc.fema.gov/webapp/wcs/stores/servlet/info?storeId=10001&catalogId=10001&langId=-1&content=floodZones&title=FEMA%2520Flood%2520Zone%2520

National Flood Insurance Program, "NFIP Statistics," last updated September 26, 2013a. As of October 11, 2013:
http://www.floodsmart.gov/floodsmart/pages/media_resources/stats.jsp

———, "Resources: Glossary," last updated September 26, 2013b. As of October 16, 2013:
http://www.floodsmart.gov/floodsmart/pages/glossary_A-I.jsp

National Research Council, Water Science and Technology Board, Division on Earth and Life Studies, "New Study Announcement: Analysis of Costs and Benefits of Reforms to the National Flood Insurance Program—Phase 1," undated.

New York City Administrative Code, Title 26, Housing and Buildings, Chapter 4, Rent Stabilization.

New York Property Insurance Underwriting Association, "Coastal Market Assistance Program," undated. As of October 17, 2013:
http://www.nypiua.com/cmap.html

New York State Code, Insurance, Article 54, New York Property Insurance Underwriting Association, Section 5414, Coastal Market Assistance Program (C-MAP).

New York State Department of Financial Services, "Homeowners and Tenants Insurance," undated; referenced April 10, 2013. As of October 11, 2013:
http://www.dfs.ny.gov/consumer/homeown/homeown_006_renters.htm

———, *New York State Homeowners Coverage: Approved Independent Mandatory Hurricane Deductibles: Revised as of 3/20/2013*, March 2013a.

———, "Homeowners Resource Center," updated April 8, 2013. As of October 11, 2013:
http://www.dfs.ny.gov/consumer/home_resources.htm

New York State Hurricane Sandy Disaster Insurance Assistance, *NYS Insurers Disaster Response Report Card*, March 15, 2013.

NFIP—*See* National Flood Insurance Program.

NYPIUA—*See* New York Property Insurance Underwriting Association.

Office of the Assistant Secretary for Planning and Evaluation, U.S. Department of Health and Human Services, "2012 HHS Poverty Guidelines," last updated February 9, 2012. As of April 23, 2013:
http://aspe.hhs.gov/poverty/12poverty.shtml

Office of the Governor, New York, "Governor Cuomo Announces Housing Recovery Program to Compensate Homeowners for Repairs of Damage Due to Storms Irene, Lee and Sandy," press release, September 28, 2013. As of October 16, 2013:
http://www.governor.ny.gov/press/09282013-housing-recovery-program

Office of Senator Mary Landrieu, "Sen. Landrieu Introduces Flood Insurance Reform Legislation to Fix Biggert-Waters," press release, May 21, 2013. As of October 16, 2013:
http://www.landrieu.senate.gov/?p=press_release&id=3751

PR Newswire Association, "Almost 2 in 3 Renters Lack Renter's Insurance," San Francisco, Calif., March 11, 2013.

Public Law 93-134, Flood Disaster Protection Act of 1973, October 19, 1973. As of October 12, 2013:
http://www.gpo.gov/fdsys/pkg/STATUTE-87/pdf/STATUTE-87-Pg466.pdf

Public Law 97-348, Coastal Barrier Resources Act, October 18, 1982.

Public Law 103-325, Riegle Community Development and Regulatory Improvement Act of 1994, September 23, 1994.

Public Law 112-141, Moving Ahead for Progress in the 21st Century Act, July 6, 2012. As of October 11, 2013:
http://www.gpo.gov/fdsys/pkg/PLAW-112publ141/pdf/PLAW-112publ141.pdf

RAMPP—*See* Risk Assessment, Mapping, and Planning Partners.

Risk Assessment, Mapping, and Planning Partners, "Preliminary Work Map Data," June 18, 2013. As of October 22, 2013:
http://184.72.33.183/Public/PreliminaryWorkMaps/NY/NYC/Workmaps/

Schofer, Laura, "Cuomo: State Will Compensate for 'Earth Movement' Loss," *Baldwin Herald*, October 2, 2013. As of October 16, 2013:
http://liherald.com/baldwin/stories/Cuomo-State-will-compensate-for-earth-movement-loss,50152

Stellin, Susan, "A Word to the Wise Renter: Insurance," *New York Times*, January 27, 2012. As of October 11, 2013:
http://www.nytimes.com/2012/01/29/realestate/
getting-started-a-word-to-the-wise-renter-insurance.html

U.S. Bureau of Labor Statistics, "Consumer Expenditures in 2009," news release, USDL-10-1390, October 2010.

U.S. Census Bureau, American Community Survey, 2006–2010.

U.S. Government Accountability Office, *Flood Insurance: More Information Needed on Subsidized Properties*, Washington, D.C., GAO-13-607, July 3, 2013. As of October 11, 2013:
http://www.gao.gov/products/GAO-13-607

U.S. Statute 61-193, Housing and Rent Act of 1947, June 30, 1947.

Watt, Richard, Francisco J. Vázquez, and Ignacio Moreno, "An Experiment on Rational Insurance Decisions," *Theory and Decision*, Vol. 51, No. 2–4, December 1, 2001, pp. 247–296.

Wharton Risk Management and Decision Processes Center, *Managing Large-Scale Risk in a New Era of Catastrophes: Insuring, Mitigating and Financing Recovery from Natural Disasters in the United States*, March 2008.